The Twilight of Glob

Recasting Marxism

Boris Kagarlitsky

New Realism, New Barbarism

The Return of Radicalism

The Twilight of Globalization

Property, State and Capitalism

Boris Kagarlitsky

Translated by Renfrey Clarke

Pluto Press

LONDON • STERLING, VIRGINIA

First published 2000 by Pluto Press
345 Archway Road, London N6 5AA
and 22883 Quicksilver Drive,
Sterling, VA 21066–2012, USA

British Library Cataloguing in Publication Data
A catalogue record for this book is available from the British Library

ISBN 0 7453 1586 0 hbk

Library of Congress Cataloging in Publication Data
Kagarlitsky, Boris, 1958–
    The twilight of globalisation : property, state and capitalism / Boris
    Kagarlitsky.
        p. cm.—(Recasting Marxism)
    Includes bibliographical references and index.
    ISBN 0–7453–1586–0
        1. Economic development. 2. Capitalism. 3. Economic policy.
        I. Title. II. Series.

    HD75.K33 2000
    338.9—dc21

                                                             99–046657

Designed and produced for Pluto Press by
Chase Production Services, Chadlington, OX7 3LN
Typeset from disk by Stanford DTP Services, Northampton
Printed in the European Union

Contents

Preface

This is the second volume of 'Recasting Marxism'. In the first volume I had to deal with the actually existing left and with the theoretical debates which, according to my point of view, will shape its future. The crisis of the left is produced not by a lack of 'realism' or 'ideological obsession' but by a lack of ideological vision. To overcome the crisis we must de-revise Marxism and revitalize its theoretical tradition basing our politics on class interests. However these interests themselves have to be redefined on the basis of the new social contradictions.

In the second volume I deal with left-wing strategies towards the state and nation. I am convinced that the popular argument about the 'impotence of the state' in globalized capitalism is not only wrong but deeply dishonest. It hides the use of the state institutions by the organizations of financial capital and multi-national corporations. It is precisely the strength of these capitalist institutions that forces us to put even greater emphasis on strengthening the nation-state as a countervailing force and the basis of any democratic participation.

The argument about the 'powerless state' is also a form of blackmail. If a state does anything wrong, it is going to be punished. States can't break the rules unilaterally because they will be subjected to all sorts of pressures, including trade boycott, lack of investment and technology transfer, destabilization and even military intervention. States can't change the rules together because one has to make the first step, and that means immediate punishment.

For the great majority of the world population, however, no punishment could be worse than the continuation of the current situation. Naturally, if a state takes decisive steps, it must face the risks involved. But without that, any politics is impossible.

In reality the masses in the periphery as well as in the core countries are less afraid of the punishments meted out by global capital than the middle classes, who fear the prospect of sacrificing some of their consumption. All contemporary leftist movements, however, in one way or another, are subordinating the masses to middle-class leaderships.

The new leftist movements are in the making now. It is too early to predict the shape of the things to come. However, in the third volume of this trilogy I will try to discuss the perspectives and the contradictions of the left which are emerging out of this crisis.

Answering some of the questions facing the left is the purpose of the trilogy. But most important questions must be dealt with and answered by the leftist movements themselves. The trilogy is written not just for academics but above all for the activists of the left. If it helps them to deal with their problems, if it is going to be useful in their struggles, then my mission is accomplished.

Introduction:
The New Big Brother

In 1948 when George Orwell wrote *Nineteen Eighty-Four* it was quite clear where Big Brother was to be found. While at that time big government was seen by many as the solution to the problems of postwar Europe, Orwell described the other side of the coin. Big Brother was not just another name for the Soviet system; Big Brother represented the omnipotent and omnipresent state that left no room for personal choices and individual freedoms. Big Brother was to care for, protect and lead 'the little men', or at least promised to do so; but also left them frustrated and powerless before a faceless bureaucracy.

Since then the situation has changed. With the triumph of neo-liberalism the state was dramatically weakened. Bureaucracy was either downsized or stripped of many powers. But 'the little man' does not feel any more free or secure, and the feeling of frustration and fear remains.

While the state was getting weaker, multinational companies and international financial institutions grew stronger. The budgets of some companies are bigger than those of many states. Large companies now lead development and sometimes pose as caring, but they are totally unaccountable. While the state no longer tries to control big business, multinational capital exercises enormous control over the lives of people and the state itself.

Public planning is replaced by private planning. Global institutions established after the war to regulate international economy, have changed their nature. The International Monetary Fund (IMF), the World Bank, the General Agreement on Tariffs and Trade (later transformed into the World Trade Organization – WTO) were established to provide some degree of public control over the international market. Neo-liberalism turned them into instruments of deregulation. But not only that. They formulate their own agenda and impose it on peoples and states.

'National governments have ceded much of their power to a "New Institutional Trinity" – the IMF, World Bank and GATT/WTO', write American scholars Jeremy Brecher and Tim Castello. 'These agencies increasingly set the rules within which individual nations must operate, and they increasingly cooperate in pursuit of the same objectives – objectives generally indistinguishable from the Corporate Agenda.'[1]

These institutions operate the same way as the Soviet Politburo under Brezhnev. IMF and World Bank experts decide what to do with the coal industry in Russia, how to reorganize the companies in South Korea or how to mange the finances of Mexico. The greater the scale of the problems, the more simplistic and primitive are the proposed answers. Like the Soviet bureaucrats before them, the IMF officials have a single set of remedies for any ailment, to be applied everywhere from tropical Africa to the Russian tundra. They are also hostages of their own ideology (always the only correct and universal one) and of the inertia of their gigantic bureaucratic structures. Everywhere in the world they have to overcome the 'resistance of the material'. Setting aside the rhetoric of the 'free market', in practice the world has never before experienced such centralization. Even Western governments have to reckon with this parallel authority.

Brecher and Castello correctly point to the fact that this model is basically undemocratic.

> Like the absolutist states of the past, this new system of global governance is not based on the consent of the governed. It has no institutional mechanism to hold it accountable to those its decisions affect. No doubt for this reason, it also fails to perform those functions of modern governments that benefit ordinary people. It should come as no surprise that, like the monarchies of the past, this emerging system of undemocratic power is calling forth revolts.[2]

The old Big Brother is dead, meet the New Big Brother. Now Big Brother is global or multinational, but even more faceless and even less accountable than before. It is no surprise that after experiencing what globalization has in store, so many people world-wide are becoming nostalgic for the old Big Brother.

The concentration of wealth and resources is unprecedented. No dictator of the past had as much power as the people who run the IMF or huge companies like Microsoft or IBM. But this hyper-centralized system inevitably creates spectacular problems. The point is not that the neo-liberal model of capitalism dooms most of humanity to poverty, nor that the countries of the periphery degenerate into barbarism. Such 'moral' questions do not bother 'serious people'. In this system, the trouble is that the price of mistakes is becoming unbelievably high. The huge resources at the disposal of the IMF make it possible to 'stabilize' the situation after every collapse. They can go on too long with policies based on decisions that have proved to be wrong.

Socialist critics of the free market have always insisted that this system generated a tremendous amount of waste. Neo-liberal critics of central planning pointed to the fact that over-centralized systems were also tremendously wasteful. Both arguments were basically right and were proved empirically. Global capitalism as it has emerged in the late 1990s is a system that is wasteful because it is both market-dominated and over-centralized.

The world crisis that started in Asia in 1997 has revealed how great was this waste. 'True, capital's relentless drive to restructure – downsizing and "leaning" of production, outsourcing, casualization of much work, the creation of new capital markets, establishment of new trade and investment pacts – has reshaped the terrain of struggle and resistance', writes David McNally in *Monthly Review*, 'But rather than altering capital's essential dynamics and contradictions, the crisis in Asia reveals just how explosive those contradictions could be.'[3] It became clear that the model of globalized capitalism was plagued by overaccumulation and overcapacity. This 'excessive' production is accompanied by workers being badly paid, people starving in the poor countries and the decline of social standards in the 'rich' ones. Not only are human and material resources wasted, but financial resources as well. US Federal Reserve chairperson Alan Greenspan told a Congressional hearing in October 1998: 'There are trillions and trillions of dollars out in all sorts of commitments around the world, and I would suspect there are potential disasters running into a very large number, in the hundreds.'[4] Billions of dollars were spent to bail out just one hedge fund, the Long Term Capital Management. This private company managed to accumulate debts comparable to those of whole countries like Russia or Mexico. And that was just the tip of the iceberg.

Globalization came along with the spread of new technologies, with the 'information age'. Like Soviet bureaucrats in the early 1970s who thought that new technologies would make centralized planning efficient overnight, multinational companies and global financial institutions also insisted on technological change as a panacea for all ills. They did not learn the Soviet lesson that the problems of the system become even more explosive with the arrival of the new technology. Theorists of the information age speak about decentralization, 'network enterprise' and 'the network society'. Manuel Castells insists that 'multinational enterprises are not only engaged in networking, but are increasingly organized themselves in decentralized networks'.[5] This transformation is real but very limited and it can even strengthen the contradictions within the system. Many economists describe this emerging new paradigm as 'concentration of control combined with decentralization of production'.[6] The 'network society' is a utopia, at least within capitalism. Networks are growing and developing but they do not dominate the social structure. On the contrary, the dominant structures and interests try to use networks for their own purposes. That creates new contradictions very similar to those which the Soviet system faced in the mid-1960s, when it first tried to decentralize decision-making while at the same time retaining the 'leading role' of the Party.

Networks do not presuppose a lack of hierarchy or authority (otherwise the networks themselves would fall apart) – they need a different kind of authority. And they generate new interests. Capitalism gave rise to many networks, but the logic of networking is different from that of capital accumulation.

Global capital itself is not organized through networks. It uses networks, but at the same time it is centralized and institutionalized. Manuel Castells tries to convince us that there are capitalists presiding over all sorts of economies and people's lives, but not a capitalist class.

> There is not, sociologically and economically, such a thing as a global capitalist class. But there is an integrated global capital network, whose movements and variable logic ultimately determine economies and influence societies. Thus, above a diversity of human-flesh capitalists and capitalist groups there is a faceless collective capitalist, made up of financial flows operated by electronic networks.[7]

This description of a faceless capitalist network, doesn't it look surprisingly like the old Big Brother-type faceless bureaucracy? But, in the contemporary world, who makes the decisions? And why are decisions so visibly influenced by particular interests and ideas? Although the elite is faceless, it is not abstract or 'virtual'. It is embodied in the real institutions and structures where interests are consolidated and decisions are made.

This international business elite is represented politically by the IMF and the World Bank, as well as by powerful oligarchs like George Soros or Bill Gates and top executives of the multinational companies. It is extremely integrated culturally and ideologically.

The strength of neo-liberal hegemony and the relative weakness of other bourgeois ideologies (including those of 'social pact' and 'national road') is a result of this consolidation of the global capitalist class, unprecedented in the earlier stages of capitalism. However, precisely because of this consolidation at the international level, this new global elite is marginal with respect to almost every society within which it operates. This was very clear in Russia or Latin America during the 1990s, but to a certain extent we can see the same thing in Britain or in the United States. In England it was cosmopolitan globalism that undermined the old English bourgeois tradition. In the United States in 1998 'Main Street' Republicans opposed President Clinton when he asked Congress to give more money to IMF. Clinton finally won, but the opposition from the traditionalist and parochial right was far more visible than that of the left.

This marginality of the global elite explains the increasing stress it faces day to day. A common national identity or common roots were essential for every ruling class in history in order to dominate the lower classes. Once the elite is globalized while societies remain local and national, the elite finds it ever more problematic to impose their agendas on national populations. Resistance to globalization grows in Mexico and France, Russia and South Korea. In this situation the state becomes essential again for the neo-liberal elite, but only as a tool of coercion.

States have used coercion ever since they first appeared in history, but it was always justified and legitimized through 'national interests'. This is no longer possible. On the contrary, state coercion is now used as a method of suppressing national interests. The level of coercion is different as well as the level of resistance, but the problem exists everywhere.

Not surprisingly in such circumstances, the left which really dares to resist neo-liberal agendas becomes patriotic. It has to defend national societies against the global elites and against the national state, which is transformed into their tool.

This creates not only new opportunities but also great ideological problems for the left. In Mexico or France there is a tradition of democratic, republican and revolutionary patriotism. In Russia or Germany this tradition does not exist or it is extremely weak. Russian nationalism was never a revolutionary force, it was always used by reactionary forces against democratic and socialist currents. There is always a temptation to borrow inspiration not only from the past but also from the right. This is exactly the case of the leadership of the Communist Party of Russian Federation, which has gradually transformed itself into a nationalist conservative formation. But that does not mean that the left must reject patriotism as an 'old-fashioned' or 'bourgeois' ideology. On the contrary, the socialist movement has to formulate new 'patriotic' agenda based on the ideas of citizenship and human rights, and its own new vision of the democratic and decentralized state.

The crisis of 1998 was the moment of truth for globalized capitalism. It is also the starting point for the new socialist project. We must continue to resist. But we must also think in terms of institutional change. We must present ourselves as the democratic alternative to the totalitarian power of the global capitalist Big Brother.

1

The State and Globalization

For Marxists, the question of the state has always been above all a question of power. Marx and Engels spoke of state institutions as a system of organized and legalized class coercion. Lenin not only saw in the question of power the main question of any revolution, but also reduced it to the seizure and subsequent transformation of the 'state machine'. By the 1970s, however, it had become obvious that the state no longer enjoyed a monopoly on power. Michel Foucault shook the thinking of the French radical intelligentsia by showing that power is dispersed, and does not by any means reside where people are accustomed to look for it. Inevitably this has been reflected in the strategy of the left.

Realizing that the state did not possess the totality of real power in modern capitalism, leftists became disillusioned with the possibilities which the state offered. But if the state does not dispose of all power, that does not mean that the question of power can be decided outside of and apart from the state. Too few leftists have posed the question of using the state as a bridgehead in the struggle for real power. Without this, any discussion of reforms loses its meaning.

Democracy and the Market

Andrey Ballaev noted on the pages of *Svobodnaya mysl'* that the main weakness of socialists has always been their underestimation of the need for links between socio-economic and political reforms. 'To put it somewhat crudely, socialism perceives the "rules of the game" of modern democratic republics as a sufficient and even indispensable precondition for its progress.'[1] In practice, everything is far more complex. The new problems of society require a qualitative transformation of the state system.

Because the capitalist market cannot get by without non-market institutions, the state as a non-commercial entity plays a key role, not only financing public bodies but also overseeing the interaction between the development of the economy and that of the various structures of the social sphere. Among Marxists in the early twentieth century a bitter polemic raged between those who saw in the West the triumph of 'pure' democracy and those who viewed the state above all as an instrument of class coercion. In essence, however, both sides merely revealed the limitations of 'classical' Marxism. It was no accident that Gramsci in his *Prison Notebooks* devoted so much space to the concept of 'hegemony' that later became so fashionable. Without a certain consent by the governed, the state could hardly perform its class function. But this means that the state system, as an instrument of the ruling class, cannot fail to take account of the interests of other social layers as well. When the institutions of power prove incapable of this, the state system enters into crisis.

The contradictory nature of the state's role is reflected in the similarly contradictory policies of the left in relation to the state. But it is not only the left that has problems here. Liberalism, that proclaims the principle of the 'small state', needs police coercion in order to put its ideas into practice. It seems strange at first glance that liberalism, as an ideology of the bourgeoisie, should attack the bourgeois state. But this contradiction is illusory; liberalism is aimed against the non-bourgeois elements in the bourgeois state. Liberalism continually calls for a reduction to the minimum of the role of those institutions that are not linked directly to the defence of the capitalist order. In so doing, it constantly destabilizes this order.

The institutions of the state ensure the historical continuity without which the legitimacy of power can seem very dubious. This is why Britain and the Scandinavian countries have retained the monarchy, even though their political systems have become models for many republics. If kings and lords constitute a link with the pre-capitalist past, the welfare state provides a link with the future. Neo-liberal reaction is aimed at breaking this link. If history comes to an end, the future will never happen. And to ensure this, it is necessary to take the appropriate measures.

The representatives of the social sphere – those working in public services, science, education, etc. – do not like the state, but their situation becomes still worse when state institutions are weakened. Intellectuals cannot stand bureaucrats, but they constantly appeal to them for help. Without the state the secular intelligentsia cannot exist. The clerical intelligentsia can, as is proved by the history of feudalism. But the average modern intellectual is not prepared to enter a monastery.

The social sphere, which plays an increasing role in the life of humanity, cannot develop outside the state, but at the same time the structures of the state are quite unsuited to it. 'For the present', noted Ballaev, 'this conflict is more reminiscent of a contest in which the social sphere is gradually gathering strength, despite suffering constant defeats.' This conflict shifts more and more towards the regional and inter-state level, where the contradictions that were earlier evident on the national level are reproduced in a new form. Sooner or later such development leads either to catastrophe or to 'the transformation of the economic system and of the political nature of the state'.[2]

The contradiction between the theoretical need for the renewal of the state and the practical bankruptcy of the state in its present-day form spills over into the impotence of the political strategy of the left, the confused declarations of ideologues and the bewilderment of activists. A theoretical argument which is frequently invoked in order to justify inaction holds that the national state, as a central element in the strategy of leftists (whether Marxists or social democrats), is now losing its significance. The weakening of the role of the national state in the context of the 'global market' is an incontestable fact. But it is equally indisputable that, despite this weakening, the state remains a critically important factor in political and economic development. It is no accident that transnational corporations constantly make use of the national state as an instrument of their policies.

It is clear that leftists need to have their own international economic strategy, and to act in a coordinated way on a regional scale, but the instrument and starting point of this new cooperation can only be a national state. There is no need to suppose that capital can reconcile itself to radical reforms in the sphere of property. In a country where unique resources are present (and many countries including Russia, Mexico and South Africa have such resources), and where regional business interests are concentrated, even large transnational corporations will prefer to make concessions to the state sector rather than to place at risk the very possibility of their participating in this market.

In general, it should be noted that among left ideologues a healthy scepticism with regard to the possibilities of the state has very quickly been replaced by completely absurd theories in the spirit of 'stateless socialism'. In the 1950s, when socialists posed the question of nationalization, liberal ideologues stressed that property itself was not as important as the mechanism of control. In the 1980s, however, massive privatization began, leading to the destruction of the state sector on a world scale. Meanwhile, a significant sector of the left has not only failed to resist privatization, but has in practice become reconciled to its results.

The Logic of Globalizaton

For the most part, the ideologues of the left have become reconciled to an image of the state as a demoralized bureaucratic machine that is quite unable to carry out effective management, and which merely swallows the money of taxpayers. It has to be recognized that such images do not appear out of thin air. But in most countries it was not the left that created the state bureaucracy, even if the left figures in the consciousness of millions of people as its servant and defender. At the same time the right effectively exploits for its interests both the annoyance of citizens with the state, and their no less powerful demand that the state defend them against foreign threats. Such threats more and more often turn out to consist not of hordes of foreign warriors, but of mountains of foreign goods, crowds of half-starved emigrants and a mafia that is rapidly internationalizing itself – in short, the natural consequences of the economic policies pursued by the right itself.

The problem of the state becomes insoluble for leftists from the moment they reject the idea of the radical transformation of the structures of power. The established state structures start to appear unshakeable. They can either be accepted or rejected. On the symbolic level, leftists do both. Practical politics, which unavoidably gives rise to constant changes in state structures and institutions, becomes a monopoly of the right.

The democratization of power and the participation of the masses in decision-making cannot in themselves guarantee that social reforms will be successful. But if leftists, on coming to power, do not begin promptly to democratize the institutions of the state, this can only end in the degeneration and ignominious collapse of the left government.

Meanwhile, in the 1990s the very possibility of serious structural reforms on the level of the national state has been placed in doubt. Globalization has become a key idea of neo-liberalism in the 1990s, against a background of the downfall of all other ideologies. At the same time, the thesis of the 'impotence of the state', that has become widespread among leftists, has acquired three bases. Governments have been regarded as powerless in relation to transnational corporations (such as Microsoft, Ford or the Russian Gazprom); in relation to international financial institutions such as the World Bank and the International Monetary Fund; and finally, in relation to inter-state formations such as the North American Free Trade Agreement (NAFTA), which links the US, Canada and Mexico, or the bodies created on the basis of the Maastricht Treaty in Europe.

Globalization, however, is nothing qualitatively new in the history of bourgeois society. Capitalism was born and grew to maturity as a world system. It was only towards the end of the eighteenth century that national capitalism, rooted in the social structures of particular Western countries, began to develop. This national capitalism, like modern nations themselves, was not a precondition for but a product of the development of capitalism as a world system. At the end of the twentieth century, capitalism is again becoming directly global. This does not put an end to national societies or states, although these, as in the epoch of early capitalism, are in profound crisis. As Wallerstein notes:

> Modern states are not the primordial frameworks within which historical development has occurred. They may be more usefully conceived as one set of social institutions within the capitalist world-economy, this latter being the framework with which, and of which, we can analyze the structures, conjunctures, and events.[3]

While some late-twentieth-century economists and sociologists emphasize the changes that are connected with globalization, other writers stress that the processes under discussion are far from new. James Petras argues that:

> Economies, North and South, have alternated between the global and national/regional markets over the past 500 years.

In the twentieth century 'globalization' was intense until 1914, followed by a prolonged period of shift to national development during the late 1920s to the mid-1940s, followed by an increasing and uneven effort from the 1950s to the 1970s to return to globalization. The overthrow of nationalist and socialist regimes and the increased competitiveness of Asian capitalism in the 1980s has led to the current period of 'globalization', a phase which is itself today under increasing attack from within most countries, North and South. Thus globalization is not the 'ultimate' phase of capitalism but rather a product of state policies linked to international economic institutions.[4]

Petras focuses on the fact that transnational corporations also have direct precursors in the form of the merchant companies of the period from the sixteenth to the eighteenth centuries. The development of capitalism is cyclical in principle, and there are no grounds for asserting that the changes that have occurred in society by the end of the twentieth century are in principle 'irreversible'. Nevertheless, we should not lose sight of the qualitative differences between globalization and the preceding periods of internationalization of capitalism. Thanks to technological progress and victory in the Cold War, for the first time in its history the capitalist world system has really become a world system. The prediction by Marx and Engels in the *Communist Manifesto* that capitalism would overcome all state and national boundaries, has been realized in full measure only 150 years later.

Taking issue with writers who link globalization solely with the technological revolution, Petras is inclined to consider that technology has no relation whatever to this process. Globalization in his view takes its origins from a relationship of class forces that has changed to the advantage of capital. 'Technology and new information systems are just as compatible with nationalist models as neo-liberal, as the Asian capitalists demonstrated.'[5] The question, however, is not the degree to which new technology is 'compatible' with various social phenomena, but the way in which it influences the overall development of capitalism. In this sense Petras's views, despite the understandable political charge that they carry, represent a sort of sociological subjectivism. Analysing the world expansion of capitalism in the nineteenth century, Marx and Engels did not by any means consider technology to be neutral. On the contrary, they directly linked the new phases of development of capitalism to the new productive potential.

It is significant that the 'international' cycles in the development of capitalism have been linked with periods when the technologies that expedite trade and communications have been developing more rapidly than the technologies of production itself. The period of mercantile capitalism of the sixteenth to the eighteenth centuries was an age of geographical discoveries, of rapid improvements in ship design and construction (it is enough to compare the slow-moving Mediterranean galleys with the frigates of later times), of road-building, and so forth. The Industrial Revolution coincides with the rise of the national state. The appearance of Fordist mass-production technologies also coincides with the growing role of the state in the twentieth century. Production is always local; it needs a particular setting, where concrete social and political problems have to be resolved.

In the late twentieth century, despite the growth in the productivity of industrial labour, the pace of development of communications technologies has been substantially more rapid. It is here that we see the most impressive achievements of the technological revolution. This is beyond question an objective precondition of globalization. But the situation will not always be thus. The development of capitalism is not only cyclical, but also uneven. Communications technologies cannot develop at a forced tempo forever, simply because society does not need this. By the mid-1990s the supply of technological innovations already clearly exceeded the demand for them. Resistance by users to the introduction of new processors and computer systems had already become a serious problem for the firms operating in this market. The cycle was coming to an end.

The globalization of the late twentieth century is the third in the history of capitalism, but it is qualitatively different from its predecessors. If the internationalization of the economy in the period from the sixteenth to the eighteenth centuries was accompanied by an acute crisis of the state, in the late twentieth century the strengthening of the state (at least in the countries of the 'centre') and the expansion of the capitalist market have gone hand in hand. This is the essence of the phenomenon known as imperialism. In the epoch of the early bourgeois revolutions, the bases of the feudal state were being undermined. In the epoch of imperialism, by contrast, the state was quite adequate to the demands of capitalist development, having become fully bourgeois. What we observe in the late twentieth century shows that a contradiction has arisen between the present forms of the state and the interests of capital. On the whole it is not the state as such that is in crisis, but merely those of its structures and elements whose development has extended beyond the bounds of capitalism. Therefore, the present globalization is tightly interlinked with social reaction.

Encountering the phenomenon of globalization, left analysts have become divided into two camps. Some have seen globalization as an inevitable process, technologically preordained and impossible to resist, while others have viewed it as a product of the political will of the bourgeoisie, almost as a conspiracy, which can be thwarted with the help of a counterposed political will. It seems that what leftists have analysed is not the real process of globalization, but the bourgeois concept of it. The real processes occurring in the world economy have not been the topic of the great theoretical discussion, but merely the background to it, or illustrations.

Meanwhile, every attempt to examine concrete processes using particular countries as examples has prompted the conclusion that technology, though not neutral, is not all-powerful either. The new informational and productive potential acquired by transnational corporations in the late twentieth century has indeed created the preconditions for globalization, and also predetermined the success of the West in the Cold War. But the technologies are continuing to develop, opening up new possibilities, including possibilities for resisting capitalist globalization.

The 'Impotence of the State'

The thesis of the 'impotence of the state' is a self-fulfilling prophecy. A state that acts strictly according to the rules dictated by neo-liberal ideology and the International Monetary Fund does in fact become impotent. It is true that this 'impotence' is of a very peculiar kind. Anyone who tries to issue a challenge to the existing order discovers that the state remains quite strong enough to take up the struggle.

Despite the fact that international financial institutions have acquired enormous influence, they cannot pursue their policies except through the agency of the state. At the same time, the experience of Eastern Europe has shown that governments, especially left-wing ones, love to explain their own decisions as the result of 'external factors'. In fact, everything is somewhat different. The Bulgarian trade union leader Krascho Petkov states:

> Without denying the importance for eroding social welfare and workers' living standards of the structural adjustment programmes and also of the traditional monetarist approach of the international institutions, it is necessary also to note the 'services' performed in this area by national governments. The ignoring or underrating of international standards and rights, and the undervaluing of the role of social policy, are often the result of national initiatives, and not of foreign influence. In this case the governments are merely hiding behind the demands of the international financial institutions, while the latter in turn are not objecting openly.[6]

In just the same way, the leaders of the South African Communist Party explain to their supporters, outraged by the government's neo-liberal budget policies:

> The limitations of the budget should not be blamed on the minister of finance or upon the government in general. They are limitations that are symptomatic of any economy that remains hostage to powerful domestic and international private sector forces.[7]

For the left, the whole point of conquering power is to change the rules of the game, and at the same time to destroy the present complex of relations between national governments and international financial and political institutions. For many of these institutions, hostility and massive non-compliance on the part of national governments would be a real catastrophe, especially if the dissatisfied states tried to set up their own parallel international structures or to transform the existing ones. It is precisely because many radical alternatives lie directly on the surface, ready to be picked up, that banishing any thought of the possibility of new approaches on the national and international levels is a matter of life or death for neo-liberal ideology. Tons of paper, countless hours of television time and enormous intellectual effort are spent simply in order to suppress the discussion of alternatives.

The strength of the International Monetary Fund and of other international financial institutions consists above all in the fact that they coordinate their actions on an international scale, while their opponents are isolated. Consequently, the answer to the policy of financial blackmail should not be to renounce reform, but to search for allies in the international arena, combining this with a clear policy of change and with reliance on the mass movement within the country.

Inter-state associations can become agents of regulation. It is possible for the public sector and so forth to receive a new impulse for its development on the inter-state level. However, integration carried out within the framework of a neo-liberal strategy will never bring us closer to this goal. International structures created within the context of a neo-liberal project cannot simply be improved and reformed. The road to a new type of integration lies through an acute crisis and, possibly, through the dismantling of these structures. For example, the first attempts at a real union of Russia and Belarus provoked an acute crisis not only of the mongrel Commonwealth of Independent States, founded in place of the Soviet Union, but also of the Russian state itself; it became obvious that the Russian regions were demanding a status analogous to that of Belarus.[8]

An understanding of the fact that integration is essential cannot reconcile serious leftists either to the European Union and the Maastricht Treaty or to the Commonwealth of Independent States. On the contrary, it is necessary to wage an irreconcilable struggle against the present international order in the name of the principles of democratic integration. The decisive role in this struggle will be played by processes occurring within the framework of the 'old' national states.

Ultimately, all international institutions represent continuations of national states, rest upon them and are powerless to act without them. This applies to the European Union, to the United Nations Organization, to NATO, and even to the International Monetary Fund and the World Bank, which at times are perceived as independent global entities. The dominant forces here are not private banks, but creditor states. In this sense the global role of the IMF bears witness not to the strengthened role of elemental market factors, but on the contrary, to the strengthened global economic role of the states of the centre in relation to those of the periphery. Even private transnational companies live in symbiosis with the state; without government support they could not maintain and develop their complex global structures. They need the military strength of the state to preserve the complex rules of the game, and to defend their interests. While skimping on the social sphere, governments are forced to spend greater and greater sums on international punitive expeditions.

The Weakness of Globalized Capitalism

Globalization makes companies not only larger, but also more complex and often more vulnerable. This is why the demand is voiced for the standardization of laws, for introducing uniform social norms and for opening markets. It is untrue that transnational capital does not need the state. Without the participation of the state transnational capital could not keep its indispensable markets open and its borders closed; nor could it manipulate the price of labour power and raw materials. Capitalism is impossible without laws, and laws do not exist outside states. Even the notorious 'international law' does not exist independently. It is imposed through the efforts of particular states, which, depending on their interests and capabilities, serenely tolerate some breaches and harshly punish others.

During the 1980s and 1990s the scale of state intervention in economic, social and cultural life has not diminished, but on the contrary has grown. Deregulation is also a form of interventionism, albeit a perverted one. Now, however, this intervention has been aimed at destroying the public sector, at reducing living standards and at removing customs barriers. Practice shows that keeping markets open demands no less activity from governments than protectionism. All that happens is the restructuring of the government apparatus and a change of priorities, as is argued in an article in *Nezavisimaya gazeta*.

However paradoxical it might seem, under the conditions of the market economy the administrative globalism of the Russian government sometimes surpasses the gigantomania that afflicted the economic structures of the USSR. It will be recalled that the exorbitant cost of the mistakes made by the Soviet managerial hierarchy was one of the main reasons for the crisis of the national economy.

Neo-liberal policies have not resolved this problem. Moreover, privatization and liberalization have placed still more power in the hands of the central bureaucracy. The 'young reformers' Anatoly Chubais and Boris Nemtsov, supported by the experts of the International Monetary Fund, have arbitrarily spent billions of dollars and have reorganized government structures as if they were playing with a child's construction set, without accepting the slightest responsibility for the consequences of their decisions. *Nezavisimaya gazeta* continues:

> In the present Russian government, the cost of an error by the reformers has reached unbelievable levels, since decisions by Chubais and Nemtsov draw tens of millions of dollars into play. Meanwhile, unlike the situation in the centralized economy of the USSR, the reformers are permitted to act without any outside control.

Immense power has become concentrated in the hands of a narrow group of people who manage the financial flows within the state. 'In Russia the formation of a monopoly on the making of decisions which affect the lives of tens of millions of people is close to complete.'[9]

Almost nowhere has neo-liberalism led to a sharp reduction in the size of the government apparatus. The case of Russia, where cutting the public sector to a tenth of its former size increased the state apparatus approximately three-fold, is of course an extreme case. Nevertheless, it is not unique. Throughout the world, while some government services have shrunk, others have grown. Cuts in spending on social needs are accompanied by increases in spending on the repressive apparatus, the privatization of the public sector dramatically increases the load on the taxation service, and so forth. In the longer perspective, a balanced budget is an unattainable goal, while the financial crisis of the state cannot in principle be overcome within the framework of such a model.

Liberals have been able to revise the priorities of the state, and these priorities can also change under pressure from workers. For this to happen, political will is indispensable, and this will is realized through the medium of power. The 'impotence of the state' is a propaganda myth. But in order for the state to be able once again to carry out its regulatory function in the interests of workers, it must itself be radically transformed and in a certain sense globalized (through democratically organized inter-state associations). Left organizations, struggling under changed conditions, no longer need only mutual solidarity but also direct coordination of their actions, making it possible to campaign effectively on the international level.

The thinking of the left on transnational companies is dominated by a simplistic idea of them as homogeneous and monolithic bodies with ideally disciplined executive structures, a clear vision of their tasks and efficient decision-making processes. This strongly recalls the idealized vision of Soviet centralized planning – only now, the structures are global and private. In reality, what happens with transnational corporations is the same as with all hyper-centralized systems, including the Soviet Gosplan: they start becoming differentiated, and interest groups, sub-elites and feuding clans take shape within them. The people at the lower levels of the hierarchy manipulate information in order to obtain decisions to their advantage from the officials higher up. Anyone who has dealings with the offices of transnational corporations in the countries of Eastern Europe hears from their employees the usual complaints against the centre: that it does not understand local conditions, obstructs work, and stifles initiative. Only the centre is now located not in Moscow, but in Washington or in Western Europe.[10]

If transnational companies are not monolithic structures, but are riddled with internal conflicts, what is the source of their political power? They are powerful above all because with the help of neo-liberalism they have been able to impose their hegemony on world capital (and, even more widely, on world elites).

Neo-liberal Hegemony vs. Democracy

From the very beginning neo-liberalism was a hegemonic project in precise accordance with the concepts of Western Marxism. The technological changes that brought shifts in the structure of society in the 1980s could not fail to provoke a crisis of hegemony as well. This crisis was used by international financial institutions and neo-liberal ideologues in two ways. On the one hand, the traditional class hegemony in the world of labour was undermined, and, on the other, the transnational corporations managed to bring a 'new class consciousness' to the world of capital, consolidating it around themselves. The differences and contradictions remain but, as in any class project, the part is subordinate to the whole, the particular to the general.

It is this unprecedented consolidation of elites that has given the neo-liberal project its astonishing strength. The various groups have continued to struggle among themselves, but within the framework of a common orientation. Changes of government have not led to changes of course, and clashes of interest have been confined to lobbying. The problem of neo-liberalism lies in the fact that its structure of dominance is inevitably superimposed on the far more complex and diverse structures of various societies. Hence neo-liberalism, without claiming to make human society united or homogeneous (this would undermine the ability of capital to practise global manip-ulation), strives to simplify the task before it, to make all societies alike, structurally similar, and thus easily understood and managed on the basis of common rules.

This runs up against the elemental 'resistance of the material'. Precisely the same rejection of an alien model undermined the communist bloc. Now neo-liberalism is using these very methods.

The economy can be global, although the significance and potential of national economies should not be underestimated. But society remains restricted by the frameworks provided by countries, just as the possibility of society making an impact on political and economic decisions is limited by the framework of the national state. Therefore the desire of peoples to retain the symbols and institutions of 'their own' states is due not only to traditionalism, nationalism or 'sentimentality', but to an instinctive understanding that if these symbols and institutions are lost, the final possibility for these peoples of influencing their own fate will be lost as well. Transnational bureaucracies are also state structures, and have quite obvious national roots. But they are not democratic institutions.

Transnational capital and its bureaucracies are marginal in their relation to any society, including even those of the countries of the 'centre'. However, they are far from marginal in relation to the state. Moreover, the state is becoming more and more an organ for the defence of these 'new marginals'. 'In reality the financial groups, the manipulators of high technology, have one common feature above all: a total absence of vision or strategy. They act on a world scale, but do not master anything', writes the French weekly *L'Événement du jeudi*. 'When the states no longer organize the social space, the true master of the universe becomes uncertainty.'[11]

Criticizing the 'old left' for being excessively oriented towards the state, and defending the new slogans of 'democratic communities' and 'sustainable development', the Finnish economist Jan Otto Anresson also notes:

> Today – despite the internationalization of the economies – the nation-states are still supposed to be that community through which people primarily identify themselves and through which they are able to make common decisions. The hollowing out of the nation-states thus implies a weakening of the possibilities to realize democratic communities.

The left cannot therefore renounce the struggle to 'reinforce the capacity of the nation-states to govern, or to create other collectives to democratically regulate market forces'.[12] Here nothing is predetermined; a serious struggle is still only beginning. The question at issue is the very survival of democracy.

There are no democratic institutions on the global level. Capital is being globalized, but not people. However cosmopolitan our culture might be, the overwhelming majority of people remain physically restricted by their conditions of daily life, bound to some particular place. There is nothing intrinsically evil in this. National society and the state will remain the level on which social change is really possible and necessary. It is quite another matter that under the conditions of globalization not only revolution but also reform cannot be successful unless it spreads to a whole number of countries. This, of course, is nothing new either. It was no accident that Marx, as well as Trotsky and other revolutionaries of the early twentieth century, spoke of permanent revolution.

The neo-liberal governments that are destroying the welfare state explain to the population that under the new conditions the country can no longer permit itself the former level of social welfare. Defenders of the welfare state recall in turn that practically all the countries, where in the late 1980s or 1990s, social programmes and regulation were declared 'impermissible luxuries', are now much richer than at the time when these measures were first introduced. In principle, such discussions are pointless; both sides are right. The irrationality of modern capitalism makes itself evident in that the accumulation of wealth by society does not in principle guarantee a happy life to society's members.

The welfare state is becoming impossible not because society has become poorer, but because its social and economic structures have changed. The Fordist model of mass production presupposed that the workers in an enterprise were themselves able to consume their own production. The national economy and the domestic market remained more or less closed, self-sufficient systems. Entrepreneurs had an interest in seeing wages grow, since this meant an automatic expansion of the market for the goods and services they produced. However, the overall interests of the bourgeoisie and the interests of the individual entrepreneur, with an incentive to economize on wages, continually contradicted one another. State regulation was therefore essential for maintaining social discipline and economic solidarity within the ruling class itself.

As Samir Amin notes:

> Regulation was strictly national. It was constructed within autocentric productive systems still largely autonomous, notwithstanding their interdependence within a world market. It worked only to the degree that the national state exercised effective control over its means of managing the national economy and its external exchanges in trading competitiveness, capital and technology flows.[13]

Amin also correctly stresses that such regulation was possible only in the countries of the capitalist centre, and that it was based on the maintenance of unequal relations between the 'centre' and the 'periphery'. This was why attempts to export social democracy to the countries of the Third World, where a different model of industrialization was being established, invariably ended in failure: 'This new industrialization was based on the deployment of Fordism without a social-democratic compromise.'[14] Economic development in the countries of the periphery created the conditions for globalization, in which the countries of the capitalist centre retained control over the movement of capital, but lost their monopoly on massive industrial production.

State borders are a particularly important element of regulation within the framework of the neo-liberal project, though this is the 'skeleton in the closet' about which no representative of the establishment wants to speak. If the movement of capital about the world is becoming more and more free, the mobility of labour power, by contrast, is limited. There is no global labour market. The frontier barriers between the countries of the 'centre' are dissolving, but between the 'centre' and the 'periphery' (and in a number of cases between different countries of the 'periphery') they are becoming more strict. From being the subjects of economic activity, workers as a result are becoming exclusively its objects, 'labour resources', just as passive and immobile a material as, let us say, deposits of iron ore. Through the same process 'social partnership', which presupposes at least a formal equality of the two sides, is becoming pointless as well.

The globalization of the economy has rendered the social democratic compromise pointless. Enterprises work for the world market, but society remains national. The growth of wages does not guarantee demand for one's own goods. The old social contract is collapsing, since it is impossible to ensure either general social discipline on the side of capital, or consumer discipline on the side of workers, who have developed the habit of spending their high wages on goods produced by the half-starved toilers in South Asian sweatshops.

The cyclical nature of the capitalist economy made inevitable the emergence of contradictions undermining the Keynesian compromise. But the same cyclical character also creates problems for the neo-liberal project of globalization. As noted by the British sociologist Simon Clarke, the globalization of the economy in the late twentieth century, as at the beginning of the century, is closely linked with an overaccumulation of capital. The paradox lies in the fact that, on the one hand, the opportunities for investing capital profitably in the countries of the 'centre' are extremely limited, requiring increased expansion into the countries of the 'periphery'. But, on the other hand, the possibilities of exploiting the 'periphery' are not limitless either, and the capital that is exported is at times not even enough to ensure economic growth. In such a situation, Clarke recalls, 'the previous phases of global overaccumulation resulted in the rise of protectionism and imperialism'.[15]

The theoretician of the left wing of the German 'greens', Elmar Altvater, argues that the left has not yet learnt to orient itself in the 'new political landscape'.[16] Instead of complaining about the internationalization of capital, they would do better to struggle for 'social regulation yielding global results [*Auswirkungen*].' Such regulation, however, is impossible on the basis of the old state methods; it has to rest on 'global civil society'.[17] Meanwhile, Altvater recognizes that 'despite all the economic globalization no world society has arisen'.[18] Consequently 'global civil society', if it exists anywhere except in the imagination of theoreticians, is not representative of real society. Only an insignificant minority of people are drawn into the various 'free associations', particularly on the world level. This slogan is just as utopian as it is elitist. Regulation really does need to become regional and global. However, this cannot be on the basis of 'civil society', but must be on the basis of democracy and civil equality of rights, something which is impossible outside the state.[19] Beginning on the local level, regulation requires a system of local self-government and national organs of representative authority. Having grown weak as a result of the process of globalization, the state, when it is forced to reckon with the consequences of this process, is capable of winning back its lost position. But even if state intervention again becomes popular, the question of its forms and class nature remains open.

'Objective Limitations'

In 1995 the London *Economist* noted with satisfaction that recent history was 'littered with examples of markets forcing governments to change policy'.[20] In reality, this seemingly self-evident assertion is a complete lie. Modern history knows hardly a single case in which government policy has changed under the influence of the 'invisible hand of the market', as a result of a series of misfortunes resulting from objective causes. Regardless

of whether a particular programme was effective or not, its implementation in most cases was stopped long before it was possible
to speak of the 'test of the market'. Government policies have
changed in response to the demands of particular transnational
corporations, international financial institutions and more
powerful states. The obvious economic failures of neo-liberal
regimes in Eastern Europe and Latin America have never led to
a correction of course. On the contrary, the more obvious the
failure of neo-liberalism has become (even in market terms), the
more resolutely its prescriptions have been enacted.

The only case in which it has been possible for theoreticians to
speak of a 'market factor' has been the precipitate fall suffered by
the French franc after the socialists came to power in the early
1980s. But the attack on the franc by money market speculators
was not caused by a decline in the French economy, but by a
clear, conscious wish to put pressure on the socialists not to
implement radical policies. In other words, it was a form of class
struggle by the bourgeoisie.

It is quite obvious that any change in any of the relevant
conditions can inspire such resistance, just as all reforms are
associated with difficulties. There is nothing remarkable in this.
All that is extraordinary is the readiness of the modern left to
give in at the first sign of discontent from the financial oligarchy,
while neo-liberal governments are quite ready to press ahead
with their policies even when these have obviously failed and
the dissatisfaction is near-universal.

The role of 'objective limiting factor' in most cases is played
not by elemental economic processes, but by the actions of international financial institutions and. . . of other states. 'The rule
of money is no longer mediated primarily by the market', Simon
Clarke notes. 'The rule of money is directly imposed on capitals
and on the state by the banks and financial institutions.'[21]

When in 1997–98 financial crisis erupted in Thailand, local
elites also hoped to use state intervention as a solution, but they
were not allowed to do so.

Looking for a lifeboat, the private sector realized that its profits
depended on government spending and that the cut in
government expenditures that accompanied a stabilization
programme would hurt it. With the IMF's demand for cutting
back government expenditures, however, this source of

stimulation for economic activity disappeared in the second half of 1997.[22]

In other words, the IMF rules were imposed on the national state, even against the will and interests of local business community.

The Italian Marxists Pietro Ingrao and Rossana Rossanda urge their readers not to forget that, even in the age of transnational corporations, governments wield enormous power not only in the military-technical field but also in the economic one.[23] The scrupulously moderate Will Hutton also reminds us that the state has a significant ability to practise regulation on the international level as well:

> Globalisation is still limited by the power of national governments and vested interests of individual economic systems. It is true that the financial markets have greater power of veto than they used to, and compel more conservative economic policies, but considerable latitude remains.[24]

On the one hand, the state and national capital are quite able to use their policies to influence the decisions of transnational companies. On the other hand, the state can influence them through its participation in international organizations. 'In a number of key areas, ranging from the regulation of capital flows to fish stocks, the individual nation state can augment its individual powers by pooling sovereignty and delegating authority to supranational agencies.'[25] Hutton prefers not to remind his readers, however, that all this would have a certain point only if these agencies were themselves radically democratized.

So long as workers, with the help of the state, do not succeed in changing the rules of the game, imposing countervailing limitations on capital, there cannot be any kind of balance, and consequently even the most moderate reformism is impossible. The weakness of the left arises from its unwillingness to use the force of the state against the bourgeoisie. The growth in influence of transnational structures requires the creation of a counter-weight. But at the same time the new situation demands the radical transformation of the state, of its institutions and of its social nature. Traditional bourgeois democracy has shown that it cannot act as a serious counterweight to transnational capital, and it is therefore essential to step outside these bounds.

The general thesis of the 'impotence of the state' deliberately ignores the fact that there are very different states in the world – Belgium and the USA, Hungary and Russia, Brazil and Costa Rica, China and Brunei. It is easy enough to observe that the economic capacities of these states are different, just as their plans for transforming these capacities are different as well. As a classic example of the fact that the state plays an active role in the globalized system, we can count the experience of Japan, and that of the new Asian industrialized states. Japanese policy here has provoked conflict with international financial institutions, but the Japanese elites have continued stubbornly along their chosen path.

> Over the 1980s Japan poured aid and investment into Southeast Asia, using its strong domestic capacity to strengthen its external reach. In doing so, Japan endorsed a market-guiding role for the state in recipient countries, and justified this role by pointing to its success in the development of Japan, Taiwan, and South Korea. The World Bank found Japan's prescriptions inconsistent with its own programmatic ideas about the role of the state, which emphasized the need for thoroughgoing liberalization and privatization. Since the Bank's ideas themselves derived from largely American interests in and ideas about free markets, Japan's challenge to the Bank was also a challenge to the US state – the Bank being an important instrument by which the US state seeks to project a powerful external reach, while having a much weaker domestic capacity than Japan's.[26]

The policy of state interventionism pursued here has by no means enjoyed unvarying success. It would be risky to present it as a 'model' for the left. The example of Japan, like the success of 'market Maoism' in China, where state planning has been combined with an open economy, merely shows that there are alternatives.

In most cases the supposed 'impotence of the state before the market' is in fact a manifestation of the impotence or weakness of some states in the face of others, whose governments have taken on themselves the role of high priests and interpreters of the 'logic of the market'. This is shown to perfection by the discussions surrounding the common European currency. At a meeting of representatives of the European Union in Lisbon the conservative government of Germany literally compelled its partners to agree to limit their budget deficits to 3 per cent as an essential condition for the introduction of a common monetary unit. No one managed to establish why the figure was 3 per cent, and not 4 or 2.5. Any such criterion, like the planning targets of the Soviet era, is a product of formal bureaucratic thinking that has nothing at all in common with the 'logic of the market'. In the view of some analysts, the only aim of the German Central Bank in formulating this unattainable demand was to sabotage the process of financial unification and to retain the deutschmark as the leading European currency. Adam Smith's 'invisible hand' is nowhere in evidence here. 'It is not the market that is deciding the question of the amount and value of money, but politics', German economists state.[27]

The financial integration of Western Europe has gone ahead using thoroughly bureaucratic methods, and featuring the traditional administrative mistakes. Describing the absurd (with geographical errors) and faceless designs for the new European banknotes, presented to the public in December 1996, one observer could not help remarking: 'If an architect were to make such sloppy mistakes when submitting a plan for a building, there is no way he would win the contract.' The profoundly bureaucratic methods employed in carrying out financial integration have also provided a clue to its economic prospects.

> What we have at the moment is the worst of all worlds. The European Union is approaching the launch date of one of Europe's most idealistic and ambitious projects in history, yet it seems afraid of public opinion. It does not augur well.[28]

The practice of liberalizing the European economy also clearly refutes the myth concerning the organic link between freedom and the market. The more the powers of the state are transferred to specialized private structures and independent (although formally state or inter-state) financial institutions, the more the sphere of democracy is narrowed. Involvement by the population in making decisions is reduced to a minimum, and once a choice has been made it becomes 'irreversible'. It is worth recalling that during the 1970s theoreticians of the 'open society' spoke of the possibility of reversing decisions as one of the most important advantages of democracy over 'communism'. In the 1990s, as recognized by ideologues of reforms in both Eastern Europe and the West, a major goal was to ensure that these reforms were 'irreversible'. Within the framework of neo-liberal strategy, euromoney is becoming yet another factor of irreversibility, undermining democracy in the process. If the population loses access to the making of decisions, the financial bureaucracy acquires independence from the population: 'Without a direct link between money and citizens, Europe is heading into a terrible regression.'[29]

It is striking how, on the international level, the capitalism of the end of the twentieth century is precisely reproducing all the contradictions and vices of the bureaucratic centralization which a few years earlier led to the downfall of the Soviet system. Is this not a sign of imminent catastrophe?

Citizenship in Decline

The institutions of popular representation are in profound crisis. This applies both to the 'old' democracies of the West and to the former communist countries which borrowed parliamentary corruption without parliamentary culture. During the 1970s European left theoreticians spoke of a transition that was supposed to be occurring from bourgeois democracy to 'advanced democracy', which was no longer an instrument of class domination. This transition has not been successfully carried through anywhere, ever. After the fall of the Berlin Wall, amid the shouts about the triumph of freedom, the reverse process got under way even in the most developed countries. From constituting an association of citizens, democracy is being transformed into a form of interaction of elites, or, to use Aristotle's term, an oligarchy.

Back in 1988 Simon Clarke wrote of a sort of 'political revolution' that had been carried out by the neo-liberals. The idea of a political revolution carried out by workers within the framework of incipient socialism, an idea advanced by Trotsky as an alternative to Stalinist 'degeneration', was arguably a utopia. But the political revolution carried out by the bourgeoisie against the welfare state became a reality in the 1980s and 1990s.

Together with the welfare state, civil society also suffered a crushing defeat.

> The increasingly ruthless subordination of civil society and the state to the power of money has accordingly led to the progressive erosion of the legitimacy of representative and democratic bodies, which are reduced to the fora within which particular interests press their partisan claims, and against which monetarism asserts the primacy of the general interest embodied in the disinterested rule of money.[30]

In many parts of the world the 1990s saw the setting up or revival of democratic institutions, but the ease with which this occurred witnessed the weakening of their role. They no longer hindered anyone, and did not place difficult problems before the elites. They ceased to exert decisive influence on the life of society, and thus no longer posed a danger to the ruling classes even in states that were experiencing serious social crises. The weakening of the labour movement aided the implantation of this 'inoffensive democracy'. But wherever parliaments or municipal organs created serious problems for the neo-liberal project, they were mercilessly disbanded, as happened with the Greater London Council, the Peruvian Congress and the Supreme Soviet of Russia. If it was necessary to shoot, the elites shot. If they had to break the law, the law was broken. If it was necessary to rule by decree, this was done. And all this occurred within the framework of 'democratization'. Unlike earlier times, the disbanding of representative organs was not followed by the installing of repressive dictatorships. In most cases new organs, more in line with the neo-liberal project, were simply established in place of those that had been abolished.

Eastern Europe is orienting itself toward Western Europe, and Western Europe in turn is becoming more and more like America. During the 1980s European political life offered a significantly richer choice of alternatives than its American counterpart. During the 1990s this situation has changed. The European elites have become increasingly oriented toward the transatlantic political model.

As the American political scientists Daniel Hellinger and Dennis R. Judd have noted, the present-day elites are interested in democracy only as a means for legitimizing their power. The political system is thus evolving in the direction of oligarchy, while elections, free discussion and the struggle between parties are turning into a 'democratic facade'.[31] A regression is occurring from a democratic to a liberal state. Will Hutton sees the same process occurring in Britain:

> Everywhere the ideological edge of political competition has been blunted. Different parties, when in government, offer similar programmes. Yet democracy depends on parties being able to develop distinctive policies that correspond to some coherent political vision. If the only choice – forced on political parties by the new power of veto of the global capital markets, which threaten a run on the currency of countries whose policies they dislike – is some variant of the new conservatism, then political debate becomes a charade.[32]

The American sociologist Christopher Lasch, in his book *The Revolt of the Elites and the Betrayal of Democracy*, has characterized the policy of the elites, aimed at excluding the masses from decision-making, as 'the abolition of shame'.[33] The integrating mechanism of capitalist democracy is being destroyed. 'Those who saw themselves losing out in the market economy saw government as a positive force working to keep them included when it came to harvesting the economic fruits of capitalism', Thurow states.[34] Therefore, state redistribution is always one of the foundations of democracy under capitalism. To a significant degree, its rejection robs bourgeois democracy of meaning, transforming it into oligarchy or an 'intra-party' democracy of the elites.

The new democracies are afflicted by the same ailments as the old. Corruption is eating away at their political institutions. Disillusionment with democratic institutions, with elections and parliamentarism, is on the rise, even in countries that have long traditions of the struggle for freedom. 'Compared to the military-dominated regimes of the past, the current civilian government seems to be plagued by an even greater number of audacious and reckless irregularities and a rising tide of suspicion over the links between economics and politics', South Korean journalists wrote in the late 1990s. 'Compounding this frustration is the fact that the same people who dedicated themselves to democratization during one of the nation's darkest periods have become just as corrupt as those whom they once denounced.'[35]

Corruption is indeed becoming a global phenomenon, and this is closely linked to the changes occurring in the economy. The defence mechanisms devised by democratic systems during the epoch of early or welfare capitalism are no longer working. New forms of graft and new temptations are appearing. As the state becomes more and more 'open' to the outside, it simultaneously becomes less and less susceptible to control by its own citizens; as a result, new opportunities for abuses proliferate. The ideology of the neo-liberal market, by destroying non-market ethical norms, also plays a role here.

What is changing is not only the style of rule, but also the institutions themselves and the norms that are codified in legislation. The most dangerous tendency in late Western democracy is the limitation of the meaning of citizenship. The Enlightenment proclaimed that the rights of humanity and of citizens are one and the same thing. Every inhabitant of a republic became a member, with equal rights, of the state community.

The restricting of citizenship rights has occurred during the liberal epoch as well. Throughout the entire history of capitalism, in fact, the principle of universal civil rights, inseparable from human rights, has come into endless conflict with political practices that have contradicted this principle. Classical capitalism, however, was characterized by a positive dynamic; civil rights were won by workers, by new immigrants, by women, and by the inhabitants of colonies and overseas departments. The principle of universality triumphed. But in present-day capitalism a countervailing tendency is starting to triumph for the first time. Citizenship is increasingly becoming a privilege, as in a slave-owning society or a feudal republic. Those who are denied it are not only new emigrants and their children, who in Western societies make up a constantly growing sector of the population. Even a significant proportion of those who formally enjoy the rights of citizenship are not in a position to exert these rights. The people who are denied citizenship are not only the poorest, but also usually the most proletarianized.

In Estonia and Latvia, Russian-speaking residents who settled in these republics after 1940, along with their descendants, have been denied citizenship rights. The European Union has criticized the Baltic governments, declaring: 'Some work needs to be done in terms of ensuring that the Russian population have full rights and a clear road to establishing those rights.'[36] But in Western Europe itself the situation is far from ideal.

Moreover, substantial differences had arisen between the Baltic republics by the early 1990s. If the authorities in Latvia took a rigid attitude to 'non-citizens', in Estonia the number of Russians who received citizenship grew quite rapidly. As well as those who managed to prove their 'hereditary right' to citizenship, about 80,000 people received citizenship through naturalization, after passing an examination on their knowledge of the Estonian language. Overall, the Estonian requirements for naturalization could even be considered more liberal than those in Germany, where a knowledge of the state language is not a sufficient basis for naturalization. The international community, meanwhile, has not censured Germany for restricting the rights of its non-native population.

Despite this, the director of the Estonian Department of Citizenship and Migration, Ene Rebane, has acknowledged that the republic is home to a large number of people 'who were born here, but who under the existing laws do not have an automatic right to become citizens'. Rebane called on these people to decide for themselves the nature of their relations with the Estonian state, and not to 'nurture a grudge' against it, especially since they would at a certain point 'inevitably have to deal with this state, even if this is simply when they grow old and the question of a pension arises'.[37] And what about the state itself, which has been in no hurry to decide its relations with roughly a quarter of its own population?

Confused and contradictory legislation, along with numerous bureaucratic requirements, have inevitably become a source of conflict. In 1996 the Estonian authorities withdrew the residence rights of Yury Mishin, one of the leaders of the Russian community and a supporter of the Communists. During a search of Mishin's apartment, security police found a red Soviet passport with an entry identifying him as a citizen of Russia. But after declaring Mishin an undesirable alien, the authorities discovered that he was 'a hereditary citizen of the Estonian Republic'. Estonian law forbids dual citizenship, but Mishin had not declared an intention to become a Russian citizen, and only the government could deprive him of his Estonian citizenship.

The matter became increasingly confused. An expert of the Estonian Department of Citizenship and Migration stated phlegmatically: 'If Mishin admits that he has dual citizenship, that means he has dual citizenship.'[38] The suspect himself refused to comment, with the result that the situation became even more confused. The opposition newspaper *Kupecheskaya Gavan'* carried a report on the Mishin affair under the heading 'Political Theatre of the Absurd'.[39]

The ideologues of the Enlightenment and of the bourgeois revolutions were convinced that the entire 'population' should consist of 'citizens'. The first anti-colonial revolts began under the slogan of equal citizenship rights. Today in the developed countries of the West, as once in the Roman Empire, only certain people can be citizens. The descendants of 'barbarians' are either without rights, or have to earn the right to be citizens through loyal service to the state. This means that the state itself no longer intends to serve the citizens.

Soldiers and Citizens

The principles of citizenship are also under threat in areas where at first glance it might seem that only 'technical' problems are involved. For example, the concepts of national security that have arisen during the epoch of globalization are becoming a direct threat to democracy. The replacing of mass conscript armies with professional armed forces, something now occurring in more and more countries, is incompatible with maintaining the principles of citizenship. Universal liability for military service has historically been inseparable from democracy. The first republics were societies of armed citizens. The American and French revolutions of the eighteenth century made a popular militia and mass conscription into the army the basis of their defence. The First World War showed that the creation by an authoritarian regime of a mass popular army was a move fraught with revolution and possibilities.

Mass armies have been typical of totalitarian regimes as well. This is no accident; as phenomena, democracy and totalitarianism are closely akin. Both are anti-elitist, with their origins in the attracting of the masses into politics. But the late twentieth century is marked not only by the widely celebrated victory of democracy over totalitarianism, but also by the counter-offensive of the elites against democracy.

As the sociologist Georgiy Derlug'yan has observed, the new armies are becoming more and more like the armed bands of the late feudal era. 'Even in purely outward terms, we are seeing a return to pre-Napoleonic times; this is the meaning of the reappearance of hired professional armies and of individual armour (though the latter is now made from composite materials).'[40] In theory, the need for a professional army is explained by the increasing complexity of the technology employed. But this explanation does not stand up to criticism. In the first place, technological innovations can make weapons not only more complex, but also easier to use (the Afghan *mujaheddin* made highly effective use of anti-aircraft rockets). Second, modern technology can equally be used to improve and bring up to date the weapons of a mass army. The real cause of the shift is quite different, as Derlug'yan also explains: the armed forces of the West are destined to carry out new functions, to become 'world police'.[41]

If the national wars of the past (including wars of conquest) had clear goals and were fought against familiar adversaries, international police operations are 'special' not so much because they require special methods as because their aims are not fully understood by society and, most importantly, because these operations are not perceived by society as being of its own doing. Even if society passively supports military actions (as during the war in the Persian Gulf and the bombing of Bosnia), mobilizing the population and consolidating society on this basis is impossible. The interests of transnational corporations in remote regions are not fully clear even to important sectors of the bourgeoisie, and still less are they recognized as corresponding to these sectors' own interests.

Placing its faith on professional police forces, the neo-liberal state does not become stronger. High-technology equipment is not a mark of strength, but represents an attempt to make up for the weakness that flows from the impossibility of using a mass army. The more complex the system, the more it is vulnerable, not simply to the blows of the enemy, but also to the constantly increasing likelihood of organizational and technical breakdowns, professional errors and so forth. From this also stems the fear, well known to historians of the seventeenth and eighteenth centuries, of using expensive forces in conflicts fraught with the danger of heavy losses. The war between NATO and Yugoslavia in 1999 revealed all these weaknesses. But this was not the first time in history when 'backward' warriors successfully resisted the force of sophisticated military technology. From the time of the late Middle Ages, professional armies have regularly suffered defeats at the hands of citizen-soldiers. The English longbow of the epoch of the Hundred Years' War was much less 'technological' than the Italian arbalest, but the detachments of English yeomen gave the French professional army no chance. Then when the French army under the leadership of Joan of Arc itself became a popular force, the situation changed dramatically. The Hussite militia defeated the finest knights of Europe, while the Russian volunteers of Minin and Pozharskiy drove the Poles from the Kremlin – after the 'professionals' among the Tsar's forces had simply fled.

If professional armies in the countries of the centre become police forces, in the countries of the periphery and semi-periphery modern-day feudal militias arise on the same basis, and can easily be used against one another. Where, as in Russia, general liability for military service remains, the army is divided into elite professional units and a mass of downtrodden recruits who serve not even as cannon fodder, but simply as slaves for the military elite. Under such conditions neither the slogan of 'defence of the fatherland', nor traditional anti-militarism can meet the needs of the left. The primary aim has become the struggle to stop the armed forces being turned into a modern version of a feudal levy, or into a local detachment of the 'world police'. This means returning to the traditional idea, from the time of the early bourgeois revolutions, of the army as an organization of armed citizens.

Modern society needs changes no less far-reaching than during the era of the great European revolutions of the seventeenth to the nineteenth centuries. What is required is not only social revolution, but also a fundamental change in perceptions of the state and society. Because of the complexity of modern society, radical approaches are rejected as unrealistic, but this complexity is itself among the causes of the present-day crisis. Increasing complexity is a sign that a civilization is in a Spenglerian impasse. The social hierarchy of late feudalism was more complex than the bourgeois hierarchy. On the one hand, the system of estates still existed; on the other, objective factors necessitated a search for ways of drawing representatives of the Third Estate into political life. Alongside the old nobility in England, a new one had appeared; alongside the 'nobility of the sword' in France, there was now the 'nobility of the gown'. Numerous privileges and liberties had been added to the system of mutual obligations. But the more complex and confused the social system became, the less effectively it functioned. Complexity is not necessarily a virtue. The task of a social revolution is precisely to carry out a radical simplification. The false choice imposed by the liberals of 'more state or less state' has to be rejected. What is now required is neither a reduction nor a broadening of state participation, but its radical transformation; a different state.

The crisis of citizenship cannot be overcome in isolation from the social crisis to which it has given birth. The question of what to do with the institutions concerned is insoluble unless the social relationships are profoundly altered; what is necessary is to change the nature of the state in social, not just 'civic' terms. This also implies extensive institutional change in the spirit of 'radical democracy', but much more than simply that.

Towards the New State

Paradoxically, the collapse of the old model of the state under the pressure of globalization is opening up prospects for a radical reform of the institutions and structures of power. The journal *Viento del Sur*, which is close to the Zapatistas, wrote that the neo-liberal experiment had given birth to such a profound crisis of the Mexican state that neither a change of government nor electoral reform would any longer be of help. The crisis could be solved only 'with the overcoming of this state form through a new social pact that establishes a different state'.[42]

This applies not only to Mexico. The entire capitalist periphery (and not only the periphery) is faced with the need to establish a new state system, based not on national self-assertion but on democratic participation, on the political self-assertion of society itself.

Very briefly, neo-liberalism and economic globalization as they are now operating can only be combated if in every nation-state the majoritarian society creates a political regime that serves its interests and which guarantees that this society can ensure (and not merely influence) the choosing of the public policies needed for the prosperity of the majority. In order to turn back the perverse process of neo-liberalism and economic globalization, it is not enough simply to win control over governments through the action of political parties; it is necessary to substantially modify the democracy of elites that has held sway within capitalism (when there has been democracy at all), and which includes the party leaderships. The political system has to ensure that society is always present and watchful, so that the government, however legitimate it might be, acts in the real interests of those it represents. Only if popular society wins control over the terrain that corresponds to it in each country, including in the countries that provide the base for the huge corporations that dominate the world economy, will a struggle against neo-liberalism and economic globalization be possible on a planetary scale.[43]

In other words, the strategy of the left has to consist not of defending the old state, but of using the crisis of this state to ensure that the basis for new institutions is laid both on a national and also on an international, inter-state level.[44] What is required here is an all-permeating democratization that encompasses not only the structures of political power, but also the institutions of social security; self-government; the public sector; and last but not least, the mutual connections between these various structures and institutions.

The traditional argument of radical democrats has been that liberal democratic institutions are good, but that it is possible and necessary to expand the sphere of freedom still further. In the late twentieth century this line of argument has lost its earlier force. It is necessary to overstep the bounds of the traditional institutions of formal democracy not because we can in theory create something better, but because these institutions in their earlier form no longer work in any case. If the left does not take on itself the task of radically reforming the state, then this goal will sooner or later be urged by the radical right. If democracy does not affirm itself as an extra-market and to a significant degree anti-market system, the masses will follow those who call for restricting the elemental forces of the market in the name of authority, hierarchy, the nation and discipline.

In the epoch of globalization, capitalism has become more destructive and dangerous than ever. The question is 'not whether we can expect a better or worse world from the global market, but whether we have to expect the world at all', the British economist Alan Freeman wrote in the Australian journal *Links*.[45] However, it is precisely globalization that creates the prospects for a genuinely international and universalist left movement, for the rethinking and refounding of state institutions – in brief, for radical reforms on an unprecedented scale.

The global capitalist crisis, which started in 1998, forced even the neo-liberal mainstream to change its attitude towards the role of the state. Experts of the International Monetary Fund suddenly declared that 'certain types of capital controls may be justified in some circumstances'.[46] American businessmen agreed: 'Maybe some sort of protectionism makes sense for Russia.'[47] The state must use its strength to overcome the crisis of the market. 'If that means instituting wage and price controls, or renationalizing basic industries to ensure supplies and employment, so be it.'[48]

At the same time Social Democrats started talking about global regulation, internationalized Keynesinanism and 'new structures aimed at increasing world currency stability'.[49] However, it is more than clear that no international regulation will work unless it is based on the national and regional bodies. If it is not, the rules and decisions made by international bodies simply will not implemented. And no democratization of international relations is possible without democracy at the level of a nation state.

The destinies of capitalism and democracy have finally parted company. In this situation, it is leftists who are the guardians of democracy. But the majority of left-wing politicians see their mission as consisting solely of maintaining and defending parliamentary institutions and the constitutional rights of citizens. This is essential, but it is quite inadequate. Such a defensive policy is doomed. Only if we realize the anti-capitalist potential of democracy can we win this struggle.

2

Is Nationalization Dead?

The idea of state property used to be one of the few that united socialists of diverse currents. British labourites, German social democrats, radical activists of national liberation movements and Soviet communist ideologues agreed that state property was an essential element of socialism. They argued about its scale, about its forms of management, and about its links to the market and private enterprise. But from the time of Marx, the connection itself between state property and socialism represented the unshakable basis of left ideology.

'Socialized' Private Property?

The belief in the public enterprise was shaken among the left in the 1990s after the fall of the Soviet Union. Right-wing social democrats have never been enthusiastic about nationalization. The new situation has allowed them to affirm in theory what had already become a norm of their political practice. But even radical leftists try to take their distance from the compromised idea of nationalization. Perry Anderson notes that nationalization 'was not invariably inefficient, but it brought no meaningful increase of either democracy or equality to the enterprises under public management. If the existing property relations are ever to be altered, it is clearly not by this route.'[1] As an alternative he suggests various forms of stakeholding capitalism and workers' cooperatives. The ideologues of the German Party of Democratic Socialism, the brothers André and Michael Brie declare that the time of the old ideas of state property has passed.

> Instead of nationalization and instead of privatization we want steps to true socialization through a complex of societal and economic changes: through strategic parameter planning of state and society; through a co-determination model that goes beyond parity co-determination, among other things; also through public oversight councils, in which alongside

proprietors and work crews there would also be the representation of municipalities, parliaments or social and ecological movements; through a land-use right that ends speculative profiteering (e.g. through the splitting of rights of property and of use); through the maintenance and broadening out of municipal property; through the putting on an equal level [*Gleichstellung*] and purposeful furthering of cooperative property; the limiting of the power of large banks and other financial institutions through the democratic control of the Bundesbank and through taxing of international speculative profits; through the broadening out of the possibilities for public legal access and influence also in other areas. We want immediate social, but also state, intervention into the private disposition over property (national and international) in all instances in which conditions of existential importance for people, society and nature are threatened: the outlawing of atomic weapons, of arms exports, of heavy weapons production; the outlawing of the production and use of ecologically harmful products (as has been partially achieved after years of struggle in the case of asbestos and freon); the abandonment of atomic energy; the abolition of commerce in the health sector, in education, science, culture and housing. Each of these steps requires social struggles, emancipatory movement, the change of political and social relations of forces and the institutionalizing of counter-forces, the engagement of victims. Socialization which can in such a way be introduced and realized could in our opinion be a real alternative. It could enable the domination of social goals, such as social justice, ecology, solidarity and cultural development, over against private-profit orientation, without wanting simply to abolish entrepreneurial and private interest as well as the market.[2]

How does such a concept of socialization differ from social-democratic regulation? Here the brothers Brie have a clear answer: they do not believe in gradual evolution. Unlike right-wing social democrats, they recognize that new forms of management and a new relationship of forces will not arise except as a result of acute conflict and a clash of interests. But it remains incomprehensible why the forms that become consolidated as a result of social conflict should be those of indirect socialization, rather than the most barbaric forms of private or, for that matter, state property. It is also quite unclear how these deliberately less radical approaches of which the brothers Brie and Perry Anderson speak would lead to more radical changes, which could not be achieved through nationalization.

Although the brothers Brie take a very critical attitude to social democratic 'new realism', their formulation has a certain amount in common with the ideas of Tony Blair, the leader of the British labourites in the 1990s. Demanding the repeal of the old text of Clause IV of the Labour Party statutes, Blair also referred to the failure of Soviet nationalization and to the weak aspects of nationalization in Britain. The new version of Clause IV promised instead of nationalization 'a dynamic economy, serving the public interest, in which the enterprise of the market and the rigour of competition are joined with the forces of partnership and cooperation to produce the wealth the nation needs'.[3]

With regard to this the left-wing commentator Jim Mortimer remarked that the labourites had also made constant efforts to combine these principles, but that the degree of success had been less than with nationalization:

> During the three periods of Labour government since 1945 the public sector was extended as part of the effort to promote industrial recovery. Labour's efforts to gear the private sector to national needs, through 'partnership and cooperation', were less successful. Ultimately the private boards of directors followed their own profit motivation.

Some of the projects that were implemented by Labour governments appear quite radical by today's standards: Development Councils, created between 1945 and 1951 with the participation of entrepreneurs, trade unions and independent representatives of the public; and the 'National Plan' of the years from 1964 to 1970, which foresaw the same kind of collaboration, involving long-term agreements with private capital on strategic tasks and social priorities. But even in those cases where the government's policy of reform did not collapse completely, such projects did not justify themselves. Mortimer states that it is impossible to force private capital to engage in collaboration so long as 'the commanding heights of the economy' are in its hands.[4]

Even the 'new realist' Will Hutton, who is profoundly convinced that practising social partnership within the framework of stakeholder capitalism makes nationalization unnecessary, admits: 'There is a powerful case for natural monopolies like water and gas distribution to be taken into public ownership as it becomes increasingly clear that regulation alone cannot deliver the public interest.'[5] He also considers that, in order to democratize the state and decentralize power, it is essential to create 'a framework of regional public banks reporting to the Central Bank, whose chief executives would be appointed by the elected parliaments of the appropriate region'. This Hutton calls 'the republicanisation of finance'.[6]

Talk of the efficiency of the nationalized sector, in Hutton's view, makes no sense in isolation from the question of the social nature and structure of the state. 'The conservative state guaranteed the ultimate failure of public ownership.'[7] In other words, the failure of earlier nationalizations was due not to 'the inefficiency of state management in general', but to the vices of particular state institutions, vices which also made their effects felt in other areas of life, including those in which private property predominated.

It is quite clear that the brothers Brie call for a more radical version of the transformation of the capitalist enterprise than the 'new realists'. But how is it possible to hope for success if even the more moderate variants of such a strategy have been frustrated by capital? The more 'delicate' and refined the means of social regulation that are suggested on the left flank, the more simple and crude are the methods through which capital asserts its interests. The more intricate and beautiful the projects, the more utopian they are. The main shortcoming of 'soft' socialization is that it never happens. To alter the relationship of forces in society, it is necessary to use very simple and crude means that will later permit the use of a whole arsenal of 'refined' and 'up-to-date' methods. The field has to be cleared, and the old rules of the game have to be changed. Any serious attempt to put a moderate programme into effect will engender the need for more radical measures, including the broadening of the state sector.

Self-management Alternative

The desire of many socialists to suggest an alternative to private property, along with their retreat from the compromised idea of nationalization, made the idea of collective workers' property extremely fashionable in the early 1990s. In the West this trend clearly owed a good deal to the postmodernist critique of 'universalism', while in Eastern Europe the left was simply in mortal fear of being accused of wanting to return to the times of Stalin.

After losing political power in Nicaragua, the Sandinistas managed to carry out a broad privatization of state enterprises 'in the interests of the workers'. At the same time, official villas and cars were privatized to the advantage of members of the party leadership. The position of the workers did not improve radically as a result of this, though it did not get worse either. But a whole layer of 'left entrepreneurs' arose. As recognized by an American researcher who supported this practice, the members of this layer 'provide a stable funding base for social and political struggles'.[8] Unlike the old state sector, this cooperative sector is not only free of the need for constant defence from bourgeois attack, but also allows the left political elite to feed at its expense. This in turn inevitably transforms left-wing deputies and officials into lobbyists for particular enterprises. Politics becomes professionalized, and the role of activists diminishes. The most ironic aspect is that the development of the cooperatives still does not do away with the need for a state sector: 'Those on the Left who advocate this strategy understand that, to succeed, these new cooperatives will ultimately require support from the state.'[9] Now, however, when the state sector has been reduced to a minimum, it is becoming unclear why the state, suffering from shortages of capital and expertise, should use its remaining strength to support 'politically sympathetic' cooperatives instead of developing its own enterprises, concentrating its resources in a few strategic areas. Why, in general, should support be given to cooperatives, and not to municipal or, for that matter, private enterprises? On the overall social level it makes no difference whether a productive facility belongs to one person or to a group of people, if it does not belong to the community as a whole.

In the United States there has been a significant expansion of Employee Stock Ownership Plans (ESOP). Cooperatives have become a real economic force in the Scandinavian countries and in Italy. But the most valuable example of collective entrepreneurship is unquestionably provided by the activity of the Mondragon cooperative group in Spain. The founder of the movement, Jose Maria Arizmendiarrieta tried to avoid the errors of earlier cooperatives which tried to create their own world based on the principles of solidarity. Everything began with one cooperative. By the 1990s the Mondragon federation included about 200 worker-managed firms, and had its own investment bank, insurance company, and technological, research and training centres.

Many writers are convinced that the Mondragon model represents a step toward 'a revolution without violence and built from below', arguing that it involves not simply a different type of organization of production, but also a new approach to the economy, in which the social tasks of development are made a priority and 'the indivisibility of freedom and community' and 'unity in diversity' are able to triumph. Mondragon is also a symbol of a new approach to the technology of 'ecological post-modernism'.[10] Finally, the Mondragon group has shown that all these radical principles are compatible with economic efficiency. But has the nature of the Spanish state changed as a result? And is the Mondragon movement not oriented according to general parameters of success and efficiency that are set by the logic of capitalism? The ideologues of self-management have preferred not to think of such matters.

In reality, the history of Mondragon provides a quite unambiguous answer to these questions. The rapid growth of the cooperative groups in the 1950s and 1960s occurred simultaneously with the general rise of the Spanish economy and with the modernization of Spanish capitalism. When the Spanish economy in the mid-1970s reached its limits of growth, and entered into a period of crisis, difficulties arose in Mondragon as well. The economic crisis in the cooperative community led to a rapid sharpening of social contradictions. In June 1974 a strike took place in the oldest enterprise of the group, the Ulgor cooperative, and was met by the management with a lockout.

Following the strike the Mondragon leaders took steps to try to ensure that nothing of the sort happened again. Management was democratized, and the technologies used were changed to a degree. But these steps were only partly effective. In a detailed study of collective enterprises, Andrey Kolganov notes that the success of these measures was impeded by the resistance of management, which was not ready to switch to new methods, and which was also forced to deal with numerous problems caused by the general economic crisis in the country. Such behaviour by managers is entirely natural and inevitable under the conditions of capitalism.

Researchers who take a critical attitude to the Mondragon experience consider that in fact the participation of workers in the management of the cooperatives is as fictitious as it was in the Soviet collective farms. The managers, unlike the majority of workers, possess the information that is essential for decision-making. In the enterprises there are no trade unions or other workers' organizations that are independent of management, since such organizations are considered to give rise to 'unnecessary conflict'.[11] Members of the cooperatives who disagree with the majority are not only subject to strong moral pressure, but risk being expelled from the collective. Losing your job in the Mondragon system means losing your means of subsistence; in the little Basque towns, there are simply no other employers.

Meanwhile, analysis of the Mondragon system shows that there are signs of a transition from cooperative-group to communal property. This is the secret behind the success of the Mondragon experiment, and the reason why it remains unique. The cooperators have managed to create not only a new economy, but also their own ersatz state with its own schools, hospitals and housing construction, as well as its own banking system and systems of social welfare and job retraining. This ersatz state can exist in one remote Spanish province only so long as it does not undermine the bases of society. In addition, researchers note a close connection between the Mondragon project and the idea of Basque statehood: 'The people who have really concentrated the management of the cooperatives in their hands skilfully manipulate the national feelings of Basque workers.' National solidarity serves as the final argument when other means of persuasion are ineffective. 'To be with the management means to defend the Basque Country.'[12]

Even if the real practice at Mondragon were significantly more democratic, it would still be necessary to acknowledge that while a self-managed economy can develop within the framework of capitalism, it remains marginal. In Spain, the spread of the Mondragon group's experience outside the Basque Country has been insignificant. Mondragon is an exception that cannot serve as a model. It merely confirms the harsh general rule.

Summing up the Mondragon experience, Kolganov recognizes that 'a cooperative operating under the conditions of the market economy inevitably acquires various traits characteristic of capitalism'.[13] Of course, a collective enterprise differs in many ways from a classical capitalist firm. This is the 'competitive advantage' of cooperatives, which allows them to achieve success. Present-day capitalist society, Kolganov writes, permits the effective use of essentially non-market criteria of economic activity, but 'only within the general bounds of the market system'. This predetermines the difficulties of collective enterprises, which 'run up against the contradiction between their own internal criteria of activity and the external criteria imposed by the market'.[14]

It is impossible in principle to develop your own criteria of success on the level of an enterprise or even of a group of enterprises. The achievements of Mondragon are the same as those of any well-managed capitalist company. Such companies cannot and should not take on the task of implementing structural reforms on a national or regional level. They have no relationship to the overcoming of the global environmental crisis, or to the redistribution of resources between countries and sectors of the economy. Ultimately, they cannot ensure economic democracy on the scale of society as a whole. They merely act within the framework of rules which are defined by the development of modern capitalism and of the state.

The 'Mondragon model' is especially valuable from the point of view of the theory of self-management, since it is the only unquestionable success among numerous failures and half-failures. It is significant that 'state socialism' and 'municipal socialism', despite all the defeats they have suffered, have a much more positive record.

Collective Property

The changes in the countries of Eastern Europe during the 1990s have shown once again that in real life things are very different from the way theoreticians of self-management would want them to be. In Russia and Ukraine the drawing of massive numbers of workers into privatization was an aspect of the policy of the elites, and a means of mobilizing mass support for the neo-liberal project. Workers became shareholders in substantial numbers of enterprises, and at times even became the owners. But where a controlling packet of shares finished up in the hands of the labour collective, this was followed neither by a rise in efficiency, nor by an improvement in the position of workers, nor a more just distribution of wealth. 'At the big enterprises that were purchased by their labour collectives, nothing has changed or there have been changes for the worse', states the Ukrainian economist Mikola Chumachenko. 'The proportion of funds spent on consumption has increased, whereas the proportion represented by investments has decreased.'[15]

In essence, the transition from state to collective-labour property has served merely as a cover for the seizure by management and by private financial groups of control over enterprises, as well as for managerial irresponsibility and for intensified exploitation of the workforce. The involvement of workers and the division of property were indispensable if the impression of mutual benefit was to be created, and if resistance to privatization was not to arise. Collective property enterprises in America and Western Europe also constantly disappoint their supporters.

Kolganov recognizes that property rights often remain merely nominal, that ESOP enterprises 'by no means necessarily guarantee the transfer of real control and manaagement to the hands of workers either', and that the economic results recorded by these enterprises are 'contradictory'.[16] Other writers note 'financial swindles and manipulation of the votes of workers', and also attempts by the private sector to use collective property to its advantage. However, this does not prevent the ideologues of self-management from asserting that, thanks to collective enterprises, 'an opportunity is opening up to transform property relations, taking into account the interests of the workers themselves'.[17]

Meanwhile, it is by no means the interests of workers that is the principal motive force in the development of the collective sector. Not only does the transformation of workers into owners fail to overturn the logic of capitalist exploitation; on the contrary, it extends it to its very limits, transforming the 'external' contradiction between labour and capital into an 'internal' one, replacing the discipline of hired labour with the far harsher principle of self-exploitation. In the Mondragon cooperatives the worker-owners are forced to limit their own incomes in the name of accumulation. They receive in their hands only a wage, as in any capitalist enterprise. Part of the profits are placed in special personal accounts which the workers cannot use at their discretion until they leave the enterprise or retire. As much as 20 per cent of the accumulated funds may be withheld. Economists note that this allows the management 'to restrain the growth of wages under the pretext of the participation of the workers in the profits of the enterprise, and to use according to their own judgment and in their own interests funds which in theory belong to the workers'.[18] The conclusion is irresistible that for a particular person a cooperative enterprise, subject to the same logic of the accumulation of capital, may turn out to be a much harsher exploiter than a private capitalist or a state company.

A collective enterprise cannot escape being dependent on external investors. Under present-day conditions an enterprise and its labour collective cannot in principle constitute a strategic investor, since they have neither the resources nor the information. Both these requirements can only be accumulated at a higher level – that is, by investment banks, large corporations or the state. This is recognized by several theoreticians of self-management. 'The main thing that is still unclear', Kolganov writes, 'is the mechanism of economic coordination in collective associations whose size exceeds a few tens of thousands of people. How can the principles of collective property and self-management be realized on this level?'[19] Kolganov acknowledges that at a certain stage cooperatives reach their 'limits of growth'. If they exceed these limits, he sees cause to fear bureaucratization and the growth of the contradictions between managers and workers. Ultimately, Kolganov pins all his hopes on state regulation.

The more radical Vadim Belotserkovskiy declares that for the effective development of the self-managed economy it is necessary to establish Chambers of Producers which 'should possess supreme legislative and supervisory powers in the economy, including the right to confirm and remove all economic ministers'.[20] In addition, Belotserkovskiy proposes that

Mutual Aid and Development Funds should be set up under the control of these chambers, and that money from enterprises and the state should be compulsorily diverted into these funds. Without this, Belotserkovskiy argues, self-management will remain a utopia.

It can easily be seen that in Belotserkovskiy's model a fusion takes place between the self-management system and the state, while the state itself acquires corporative traits. The real owners of capital are not the workers but their corporations, which are closely linked to the state. Will the producers be able to control the various chambers and funds? The answer is plain: to the same degree that they are able to control the state.

Under capitalism every investment decision is made independently, and capital is dispersed between owners and companies, but this does not mean that capital in itself ceases to exist or to subject individual entrepreneurs to its logic. The transition from individual to collective entrepreneurship basically changes nothing; in both cases we are simply dealing with corporations. The key idea of socialists has always been to put capital under the control of society. Of society, and not simply of the producers. In its pure form productive democracy is just as elitist and anti-humane as any other 'democracy of the elect'. Moreover, it is anti-environmental and anti-intellectual.

Ultimately, having an orientation to collective property does not spare us from having to make a choice between capitalism and socialism. If we choose capitalism, then the exploitation of a particular worker within an enterprise is replaced by the exploitation of the whole collective 'from outside'. Hired labour has been done away with, but that is so much worse for the workers, since it has been replaced by a feudal type of exploitation in which the workers use their own means of production, but are unable to dispose of their surplus product. This is a step backward compared with democratic capitalism, whose most important conquests have been free hired labour and the workers' solidarity to which it gives rise.

The contradiction between labour and capital cannot be resolved on the level of an enterprise or of a group of enterprises. The economic interests of workers cannot be reduced to the interests of the labour collectives. Every worker is at the same time a consumer, who needs health care, education, and environmental protection. The needs of workers often contradict one another. Integrating all these interests is possible only on the level of society. For the activity of enterprises to correspond to the real needs of society, producers must always be under control. Either this control is exercised by the 'invisible hand of the market', combined with a fully visible financial oligarchy, or the government takes on itself the same function. The theoreticians of self-management invariably disown the unsuccessful Yugoslav experience, referring to the fact that there the collectives were ultimately subordinated to the state bureaucracy. But this subordination flowed from the very logic of self-managed production, in just the same way as the other 'distortions' and 'deformations' described above.

Nor is it possible to justify collective property with reference to the need for a 'mixed economy'. In itself, the combining within society of various forms of property, management and labour organization is neither a blessing nor a goal. A 'mixed economy' may transform society, transcending the logic of capitalism, or it may represent a backward and undeveloped form of the same capitalism. This depends above all on the nature of the state, and on the role and structure of the public sector.

Along with the ideas of collective property, the idea of socializing the economy through pension funds and other collective holdings has become increasingly popular on the left. The origins of this idea lie in an initiative by the Swedish social democracy in 1975 and 1976 that has gone down in history under the name of the Meidner Plan (from the name of the trade union leader, Rudolf Meidner). Under this plan the largest companies had to convert part of their profits into additional shares that were transferred to wage-earner funds. These funds would control the shares through the trade unions. The surplus from the funds was to go to the development of the pension system. Under a 1984 law these funds were made regional, which was supposed to aid in the decentralization of the economy. The results of the plan were on the whole insignificant. In the view of experts:

> most of the employee investment funds behaved like ordinary pension funds; they accepted prevailing market constraints, did not invest heavily in manufacturing, and did not have a long-term view. The ethos of capitalism prevailed once again, confounding the fears of all critics and, obviously, displeasing

those radicals who had believed that they would bring about a gradual transition to socialism.[21]

The Meidner Plan had a certain effectiveness in restraining the flow of capital out of Sweden, but by 1990 only 3.5 per cent of the shares of Swedish companies had been transferred to the employee investment funds. Nevertheless, Meidner's ideas gave birth to a whole current in left theory. Richard Minns in *New Left Review* argues with reference to the development of the pension funds: 'There is now a range of social ownership models which involve significant transfers of capital and steps towards new types of "common ownership". Communism may have collapsed but social ownership has inexorably, if often surreptitiously, been on the increase.'[22] In his view the politics of the left need to be oriented toward supporting and developing pension funds that promote the policy of 'social investments'. Broadening and strengthening this system, he asserts, can bring about qualitative changes in society.

Despite the self-proclaimed moderation of its backers, this approach is unquestionably more radical than the idea of 'collective-group property'. The theoreticians who place their stake on developing the pension funds recognize the need to socialize investment policy in the interests of all workers, and not simply of particular labour collectives. This approach affects society as a whole, and not only particular enterprises. In principle, it can form part of a broader project of structural reforms.

Nevertheless, the limited nature of 'socialist pension funds' is obvious. The state sector in capitalist society can function according to its own principles without putting the general logic of the system under threat; to a significant degree it has liberated itself from this logic. This is why capitalism in periods of crisis has shown an interest in nationalization, and also why it has sought to do away with nationalized property when it feels confident of its strength. Social investments via the pension funds, on the other hand, are interwoven with private interests. Ultimately, this practice serves to make the system even more confused and contradictory. If the task of structural reforms is to simplify the system and alter its logic, it is easy to see that this task will not be fulfilled using such an approach.

The Mobilization Model

Critics of traditional Marxism quite rightly note that the social-ization of production via nationalization 'is a politico-juridical act which does not yet in itself alter the nature of economic rela-tionships'.[23] But they forget that without such politico-juridical acts changing the nature of economic relationships is impossible. Property relations are not reducible to juridical status, but unless socialization is consolidated politically and juridically, how can it exist at all? Attempts to create a state sector may give rise to state capitalism and even to semi-feudal relations, or may remain a pure formality. But it is impossible to do without such 'formalities'.

Nationalization is not a method for managing industry; it is primarily a means of changing the social and economic structure of society. The trouble is that any means can be substituted for the goal. Wherever nationalization is transformed from a mechanism for social change into a goal in itself, well-known problems follow. In any case, the economic results of state entrepreneurship in the twentieth century are not as straight-forward as liberal economists and their left-wing admirers assert.

The collapse of the Soviet system was linked closely to its earlier successes. The Soviet economy outgrew itself. The American economist David Kotz notes that despite all the short-comings of the Soviet system, until the mid-1980s its economic achievements were generally acknowledged. It was only in the 1990s that:

Western observers downgraded their view of past Soviet accomplishments. This was not a result of new documents emerging from hitherto closed archives. Rather there was a reaction on the part of many observers something like the following: if the Soviet system collapsed so suddenly, it must have been much weaker, economically as well as politically, than had been believed.[24]

Donald Sassoon, comparing the indices for a whole group of countries, also recognizes that societies of the Soviet type have achieved a great deal.

For instance, in 1955 Cuba had a life expectancy of 59.5 years, shorter than Paraguay, Argentina and Uruguay; and infant mortality was higher than in these three countries. In 1985, the average Cuban could expect to live until the age of seventy-five, longer than anyone else in Latin America and just short of the average American (75.9 years). Infant mortality in Cuba, thirty years after its socialist revolution, was the lowest in Latin America. Cuba's children were the best fed and the level of literacy was the highest. In the 1950s, life expectancy in China was shorter than that of India and infant mortality higher. By the late 1980s, China had made more progress in these respects than India. Even within India, the state of Kerala, run by communists for most of the years after 1957, outperformed in literacy and health indicators all other Indian states. Taking the same standards of measurement, the Central Asian republics of the USSR – at least until 1975 – did better than neighbouring Iran, Afghanistan and even Turkey.

Even when comparing the countries of Eastern Europe with Western democracies Sassoon also concludes that although in this case the superiority of the market economy over central planning became evident, this was 'not from the outset, not in the 1950s and 1960s'.[25]

The very successes of the Soviet system in the postwar period became a source of difficulty for it. Just as in the Soviet Union the population began to compare their standard of living not with neighbouring capitalist Turkey, but with the wealthiest countries of Europe, in Cuba people began to look not at Haiti and the Caribbean islands, where the population found it hard to make ends meet, but at the United States.

The centralized mobilizational system proved unsuited for day-to-day administration in the conditions of a developed industrial economy and consumer society. But it does not follow from this that the former successes should be doubted, or that the mechanisms of the mobilizational economy are completely unviable. They can work successfully where there is an objective need for them. The need for them can arise again, and in many countries is already arising.

If the state sector, even in the bureaucratized form in which it existed in both East and West by the 1980s, had not represented a potential threat to the interests of the bourgeois elites, they would not have set about destroying it so frenziedly at the first opportunity. During the Cold War the ruling elites of the West were forced to reconcile themselves to certain 'elements of socialism' as a sort of pay-off for social stability and steady growth. It was this which created the objective preconditions for the successes of social democracy. After the 'collapse of communism', such tactical concessions became unnecessary. A series of attacks on the 'social democratic model' ensued. The dissolution of the state sector began, making it absolutely inevitable that other structures of the welfare state would be liquidated as well. The rejection of nationalization signifies in practice the rejection of serious efforts to transform society. Unquestionably, the existence of state property on its own does not yet constitute socialism. It does not automatically ensure either a more just distribution of national income or a more harmonious development. But without a strong state sector, resolving all these problems is impossible in principle.

Trotsky, in his time, provided a good metaphor to illustrate this point: he compared state ownership of the means of production with the cocoon through which the caterpillar has to pass in order to become a butterfly. The cocoon is not the butterfly. Millions of larvae in their cocoons perish without becoming butterflies, but skipping the cocoon phase is impossible.

While fully recognizing the limitations of 'state socialism', we cannot fail to see the necessity for it. The numerous plans for establishing cooperatives and other collective enterprises, and also for flexible social regulation of the economy, seem very attractive. But without a strong state sector all this simply will not work. Unless the state sector acts as the core of the productive system, 'self-managed enterprises' will be starved of investment and, ultimately, will be enslaved by finance capital.

The only way to break the economic power of large finance capital is through nationalization. Alternative strategies for modernization and restructuring then become possible. Only with the emergence of a state sector is it possible to speak of serious social control over the investment process.

In his last book Ralph Miliband, the editor of the *Socialist Register*, wrote that the desire for socialism without the nationalization of property rested on a failure to understand how much socialization was involved in the other goals of socialism to which the same people theoretically subscribed. Without a strong public sector there could be neither a stable welfare state, nor 'true citizenship'.[26]

The Myth of 'Inefficient State Enterprise'

During the 1980s the myth of the inefficiency of state enterprises gained increasing currency among leftists. No one provided a theoretical proof of the notion that state-owned industries were economic failures. No one could cite statistical data showing that if other factors were equal, state-owned enterprises functioned worse than private ones. The only serious attempt to prove on the basis of facts and statistics that private enterprises as a general rule were more efficient than state ones was made in 1992 by World Bank economists, who prepared a brochure entitled *Privatization: The Lessons of Experience*. Studying twelve examples of privatization in Chile, Malaysia, Mexico and Britain, the World Bank representatives discovered that although the 'economic-financial' performance of both state-owned enterprises and private firms ranged from 'very good to very bad', there was 'considerable evidence indicating that the median point on the private enterprise spectrum' lay 'higher than the median on the public enterprise spectrum'.[27] The twelve cases selected, however, obviously do not provide sufficient material for such a sweeping conclusion. Moreover, scholars who analysed the World Bank's data discovered that most of the privatization success stories belonged to sectors where substantial growth was evident in any case. In other words, the change of ownership could not in itself be viewed as the reason for success.

Meanwhile, other specific studies yielded a quite different result. British experts, among them an employee of the International Monetary Fund, who had studied the experience of the developing countries, stated: 'Evidence to support the hypothesis of an inverse relationship between macroeconomic performance and the size of the public sector is lacking.'[28] The same experts stated that reorganization of management in the public sector was often a much more effective and 'appropriate' solution than privatization. The former World Bank employee Percy Mistry and his colleagues from Oxford, who studied the experience of three Asian, two Caribbean and two African countries in the same year (1992) that the World Bank brochure appeared, stated that privatization had 'met with only limited success', and that attempts to accelerate it with the help of political measures could be 'counter-productive'.[29]

The 'Chilean miracle' so beloved of the neo-liberal economists of the 'Chicago School', does not bear out the thesis of the superiority of private over state property. A significant proportion of the enterprises that were de-nationalized by General Pinochet after the military coup of 1973 were managed so incompetently that the government was forced to re-nationalize them. After a decade of military dictatorship the state sector in Chile reached approximately the same size as at the end of the rule by the left. Western authors described this ironically as 'the Chicago road to socialism'.[30]

In Britain, studies of successful instances of privatization showed that the main increase in efficiency occurred not with privatization, but in the process of preparing for it, at a time when the enterprises were still state property. After the firms were transferred to private hands, the new owners were not able to change or improve anything substantially.[31] The experience of Eastern Europe and Russia has been even more striking. Privatization has been accompanied by catastrophic declines in productivity, labour discipline and managerial responsibility, together with a lowering of the technological level and a catstrophic fall in productivity and general efficiency. The majority of the enterprises that were yielding profits for the state began making losses after privatization.

Paradoxically, the failure of privatization, which was presented as the sole alternative to the mobilizing model, brought such chaos and depression to former Soviet society that the question of a mobilizing model once again became pressing. But a return to the old model was now impossible; the situation had changed.

The rejection of state property in these countries, which had joined the periphery of world capitalism, was accompanied by a dramatic worsening of environmental problems at the same time as production was undergoing a general decline. In Russia the consumption of electricity per unit of industrial output rose by 26 per cent between 1990 and 1996. Scholars note that 'poverty is preventing enterprises from putting energy-saving measures into effect, despite the great economic gains to be made from these measures'.[32] In Russia and Ukraine the only source of funds for energy-saving measures is the International Bank for Reconstruction and Development, which is not a private but an inter-governmental organization.

Public Sector 'Success Stories'

It is significant that most of the 'success stories' of market trans-formations in Eastern Europe have not only turned out to be unconnected to broad-scale privatization but, on the contrary, have become possible thanks to the restrained attitude taken toward privatization by local elites. One of the few thriving firms in Russia is the state company Rosvooruzhenie, which is involved in the export of weapons. Moscow, which in the mid-1990s appeared very prosperous indeed against the general background of depression in the Russian economy, began to develop more or less successfully after the supporter of massive privatization, Gavriil Popov, was replaced as mayor by the 'social-pragmatist' Yury Luzhkov. The Luzhkov administration, though no less corrupt than that of Popov, has been able to improve life in the city while acting in clear defiance of the state privatization programme. In Luzhkov's view, people in Soviet times 'were relatively successful in making ends meet', while under the new order this would be impossible without 'a radical change of course'.[33] The city government in the Russian capital came out against private property in land. 'Under our conditions', the Moscow mayor declared, 'any talk of "the fundamental advantages of private property" turns out to be demagogy, because it serves merely as a cover for transferring the common property of the people into the hands of parasitic capital.'[34]

It is the city government that has turned out to be the most dynamic and effective entrepreneur in the Russian capital, creating new jobs and introducing new technologies. In Moscow a curious form of state capitalism, often described as 'municipal capitalism', has come into existence.[35] The list of enterprises founded by the city includes not only numerous construction firms, commercial trading enterprises, petrol stations and hotels, but even a municipal bank and, in competition with McDonalds, the Russian Bistro chain of fast food restaurants. For that matter, McDonald's Moscow and Pizza Hut are not American companies; 51 per cent of them belongs to the city. Luzhkov did not stop at this. After it became obvious that the privatization of the large Russian vehicle plant ZiL had failed, a decision was taken to transfer the plant to the municipal sector. Newspapers observed that ZiL had become Russia's 'first large enterprise to undergo de facto deprivatization'.[36] ZiL was followed by a second Moscow vehicle plant, AZLK. The press accused the Moscow mayor of 'using state money to solve the problem of employment'.[37] The strategies chosen for restoring production suffered from all the vices of Soviet administrative planning. But private capital, whether foreign or local, had proven powerless to do anything.

After ten years of the liberal experiment, the right-wing press has been forced to state that events have 'brought the slogan of nationalization back into the Russian politico-economic lexicon'.[38] It is obvious that municipal status is not appropriate for such a giant as ZiL. But when the conditions for de-privatization have ripened, and the federal government refuses to follow this course, there is simply no other choice. The ineffectiveness of the private and privatized sector in Russia has created a situation in which both industrial and financial firms have begun to be transferred to the ownership of local authorities. As well as productive enterprises, spontaneous re-nationalization has affected the area of finance. Liberal Western experts have been forced to acknowledge that the only way to alleviate the current banking crisis has been 'increased involvement by the city, regional and federal governments in the banking sector'.[39]

Regionalization of the state sector is the most attractive alternative to privatization. In carrying out the regionalization and municipalization of property, the local establishments are pursuing their own interests, but there is an objective need for this step. As the Russian economist Filipp Georgiev writes:

> On the basis of the state sector, the regional principle makes it possible to create a single economic infrastructure that links regions in an integrated economic system, and on the basis of all forms of property, to meet the needs of the country as a whole, of the regions, and of the cities and districts that make them up. This means that regional planning has to become a component part of national planning. The presence in the latter of programs and projects makes it possible to involve local budget funds and private capital in their realization, via direct and indirect methods.[40]

The decentralization of power becomes a reality on the basis of the decentralized socialization of property. Private capital is undergoing a rapid centralization and concentration not only on the national but also on the world level. Paradoxically, an association of regions can create more effective counterweights to this than a centralized bureaucratic state. The real rather than imaginary participation of workers in management can also be ensured on this basis. It is also possible on this level to resolve the contradictions between the productive, consumer, environmental, cultural and other interests of particular people.

Many late-twentieth-century writers note that the founders of socialism placed their faith not so much on the elements of socialism that had grown up within the framework of capitalism, but on the constructing of a new society, a task that would begin following victory in the class struggle. Collective property seems more attractive precisely because it arises and develops within capitalist society. However, the same can be said of the state sector. It is only necessary to make a critical study of the available experience, without restricting oneself to statements concerning the failures in the Soviet Union.

A peculiarity of the state sector is that its future depends on the course of political struggle and the relationship of class forces in society. For this very reason, however, the state sector is strategically important for any socialist and even democratic project. This struggle does not come to an end with nationalization, but merely takes on a different form. In any situation, private capital will pursue its own interests. If its interests contradict those of the country or of enterprises, conflicts are inevitable, however much the state might try to avoid them. In Lithuania an extremely moderate left-wing government was forced to nationalize the state-founded commercial bank LVKB after the management, which represented the interests of private investors, had brought it to the verge of bankruptcy. Business interests naturally reacted to this decision with howls of outrage, complaining that the principles of the free market had been violated. In reply, the conservative newspaper the *Baltic Times* published an editorial reminding its readers that under capitalism it is impossible to ban the state from making use of its lawful property. 'Although free market is the fad, their criticism is misleading. The government can put its money where it wants to.' While the government was borrowing money on the financial market at high rates of interest, it was keeping its funds in private banks where the rates were much lower. 'With LVKB an entirely state-owned bank now, why doesn't the government consolidate its accounts, stop loaning to the private sector and leave commercial banking to private banks?'[41]

The experience of the Czech Republic is no less instructive. This is the country that before 1997 was considered the showpiece of liberal reforms in Eastern Europe. It is true that the transition to the market economy took place here at the least cost. But this was due to the fact that the Czech leadership in 1989–97, while adopting the ultra-liberal rhetoric of the Western experts, employed completely different methods. As a result of 'large-scale privatization', property came to be concentrated not in the hands of private capital, but in investment companies and banks which in their turn belonged fully or partially to the National Property Fund (NPF). The Czech economist Pavel Mertlik notes that instead of privatization, what occurred in the country was a restructuring of state property, 'with a central role of the national government as a "core investor" indirectly controlling (via NPF and through the network of its capital shares) the spine of more or less the whole economy'.[42]

The experience of China in the 1990s also shows the absurdity of the myth of the 'inevitable inefficiency' of state enterprises. Liberal students of the Chinese economic reforms continually stress that the reforms have been accompanied by a dramatic growth in the specific weight and importance of the private sector. 'Between 1980 and 1991, the proportion of the output of state enterprises in total industrial production fell from 78 to 53 per cent, while the share of cooperative output increased from 21 percent to 36 percent, and that of private firms rose from 1 per cent to 11 per cent.'[43] In 1991, moreover, 27.6 per cent of state enterprises were unprofitable. Since then the size of the state sector has continued to diminish. However, it was the work of the state enterprises that allowed the private and cooperative sector to make extra profits. It was the state sector that paved the way for the development of the social and productive infrastructure. This also accounts for its disproportionately large outlays compared with the private sector. The losses of the state sector in China are in fact a hidden form of subsidy for the private sector. This is why the market reforms without privatization that have been implemented in China have led to a dramatic growth of private business 'from below', while the privatization in Eastern Europe, and especially in Russia, has been accompanied by an extremely weak development of private entrepreneurship.

When the Asian financial crisis erupted in 1997, Kia (one of South Korea's key conglomerates) faced bankruptcy. Finally, it was effectively nationalized, put under legal management by the government-run Korea Development Bank. As one observer noted: 'All politicians of the ruling class spoke of "putting Kia under market principles", but they didn't have any clear alternative to state intervention.'[44] A year later the Japanese government used nationalization to cope with its own banking crisis.

It is instructive that, in the cases noted, pragmatic administrators who were in no way seeking a renewal of society managed to display more radicalism than many 'left-wing' politicians and ideologues who swore their fidelity to socialism.

Privatized 'Potemkin Villages'

In the late eighteenth century, Count Potemkin, who governed southern Russia, built fake idyllic villages to impress Catherine the Great when she visited the region. The Empress was delighted but later everything came out. However, this has not prevented many administrators, both in Russia and other countries, using basically the same tactic. Western and Russian mainstream economists used it when they had to report on the results of privatization. Instead of analysing the situation they kept telling the public different success stories, some of which were simply invented and some of which were wrong interpretations of this data.

The collapse of the rouble in 1998 forced everyone to face the reality. It is not true that privatization in every single case was a failure but there is simply no reason to speak of success.

Comparing the results of the reforms in the former Soviet Union, one finds that they were worst in the countries with the highest, and by contrast, with the lowest rates of privatization. In Russia there was thoroughgoing privatization, while in Ukraine the state sector remained almost untouched until 1995. But in both countries there was a similar crisis.

At first glance one is tempted to conclude that the form of property has had very little impact on the development of production. Rejecting the extremes of 'Russian radicalism' and 'Ukrainian conservatism', one might also speak out in favour of a 'golden mean' in the spirit of the 'Czech model'. In reality, however, everything is more complicated. The slow pace of privatization in Ukraine has in no way been the result of 'conservatism' on the part of the authorities. The simple fact is that the country's economic fate, as a result of its proclaiming 'independence' and the rupture of economic ties with the other Soviet republics, has turned out to be so catastrophic that no one has been especially tempted to seize property. The Ukrainian elite has preferred to carry on exploiting the state sector financially just as its Russian counterpart did until 1991. In the cases where privatization has taken place anyway, the results have been dismal. A survey prepared by Ukraine's official institute of economics states: 'Statistical data show that following the transfer of enterprises from state to cooperative or private ownership, their efficiency has not increased.' Privatization has failed to stimulate 'either an increase in the efficiency of production, or a rise in the technical level, or an improvement in the quality of services.'[45] Aleksandr Buzgalin and Andrey Kolganov are inclined to explain the failure of self-management in Russia and Ukraine by referring to the 'traditional conformism and passivity' inculcated in the Soviet population in the Stalinist period.[46] But in fact there are also more profound reasons for the inability of the workforce to handle self-management. Industrial technology that demands discipline, subordination and a division of labour does not in principle permit workers to develop 'the psychology of the proprietor'. For this reason partial control and participation in management are often effective, but full self-management is impossible. Either it collapses, or it turns into a 'Potemkin village' behind which is concealed the power of a managerial oligarchy.

In Kazakhstan, where the disintegration of the USSR also caused an acute crisis and where the position had stabilized by 1992–3 thanks to an orientation to the 'Chinese model', the leadership of President Nazarbaev began a broad programme of privatization in 1993–94. Here pressure from the West and the influence of Russia also played a role; after the shelling of the Russian parliament in October 1993 the government of

Kazakhstan came to the conclusion that there was no alternative to the neo-liberal course. The results were not long in coming. A sharp new fall in output took place, living standards declined and the internal market collapsed.

What has occurred overall during the 1990s in the countries of the former communist bloc has not been a transition from a state-run economy to private entrepreneurship, but the replacing of a model of centralized management with a system based on mixed corporate property. This does not in the least resemble a 'mixed economy', in which private and public sectors interact. Rather, what has emerged might be described as a new type of state capitalism in which one and the same enterprise is simultaneously private, state and sometimes also cooperative, depending on its particular type of activity. State capitalism has defeated liberal capitalism. But this victory has not been the result of struggle by workers and the political opposition, but merely the result of the bankruptcy of private entrepreneurship.

The Polish economists Tadeusz Kowalik and Ryszard Bugaj, studying the privatization processes in Western and Eastern Europe and noting the efficiency inherent in private entrepreneurship, write that 'it would be wrong to conclude from this that private firms are in all circumstances better than state firms. The empirical research to hand does not offer any definite answer'.[47] The Western experience of privatization does not confirm the assumptions of liberal economists:

> Divestment of state-owned assets in market economies has not unambiguously led to lower product price, improved allocative efficiency, ameliorated internal efficiency in privatized enterprises, brought about people's capitalism, or generated better service or quality of delivery. Moreover, public enterprises were often divested well below their market value, thus generalizing sizable short-term capital gains at the expense of the state – ultimately the tax payer at large.[48]

When in 1998 the rouble collapsed even neo-liberal Western advisers in Russia started speaking about re-nationalization of the assets which were earlier privatized. The record of privatization was so bad that even free market economists agreed that in some form public sector in Russia should be recreated.

What can Nationalization Achieve?

The record of nationalization in various countries is decidedly mixed. The results of nationalization depend in the first place on the condition of the state, on its structures and on its social character. The effectiveness of nationalization, its ability to resolve social problems and speed development, like the structure of the state sector, the position of the workers within it and the degree of democracy in management, all depend on the relationship of forces in the country.

In a number of countries, nationalization has helped to solve or mitigate the problem of investment famine under the conditions of modernization, to alter the relationship of social forces, to redistribute power and incomes and to make possible a restructuring that is impossible in an organically conservative market economy. The success stories include the activity of state firms in Austria and Norway. The state sector played a significant role in the modernization of French industry after the Second World War. Despite the wave of privatizations in the 1980s and 1990s, the state sector, in the view of many scholars, remains 'the decisive link in economic policy as a whole'.[49] The nationalized banking sector served as one of the foundations of the 'South Korean economic miracle' of the 1970s and 1980s, showing the degree to which state property could operate successfully in the financial sphere, considered the holy of holies of capitalism. Even after the liberalization of the South Korean economy in the 1990s private banking capital lagged far behind that of the state. In Taiwan in 1952 the state controlled 57 per cent of industry. By the 1980s the share of the state sector had declined to 20 per cent, but this, as before, consisted of enterprises in key branches – heavy machinery, steel, aluminium, shipbuilding, petroleum, synthetics, fertilizers, engineering and semi-conductors.[50]

Speaking of the economic achievements of state enterprises is impossible without mentioning the main success story of the late twentieth century, the Internet. This gigantic information network arose and for a long time existed as an ordinary state enterprise, organized and financed by the US government. In the 1960s, the US Defense Department set up Advanced Research Projects Agency which established APRANET, the first electronic network, which later became known as the Internet. 'The fact that the Internet exists at all, by the way, is proof that government-sponsored institutions can be enormously effective', notes the American economist Nicholas Baran.[51] The existence of the Internet serves also to refute the theory that it was free enterprise that gave birth to the technological revolution of the 1980s and 1990s. As Manuel Castells recognizes, 'the state, not the innovative enterpreneur in his garage, both in America and throughout the world, was the initiator of the Information Technology Revolution'.[52] It would be more accurate to speak of the ability of the private sector to successfully assimilate technological advances that would simply never have happened without state programmes.

> It is indeed by this interface between macro-research programs and large markets developed by the state, on the one hand, and decentralized innovation stimulated by a culture of technological creativity and role models of fast personal success, on the other hand, that new information technologies came to blossom.[53]

All attempts to work out a general formula for success have ended in failure simply because there is no universal, magical formula for efficiency either. 'Making the case for public control of strategic sectors doesn't imply that privatization is invariably mistaken or that the state should fulfil all of its responsibilities directly through state bodies', notes an American scholar.[54] Depending on the specific nature of production, on its tasks and on the technological, social and other conditions, either state or private ownership may be more effective. This is why privatization has not justified the hopes placed in it, but in some cases has nevertheless yielded positive results. The method of 'blanket privatization' has resulted in the specific conditions being ignored, just as they were with total nationalization. The division of 'spheres of economic responsibility' between the social and private sectors can serve as a formula for a workable mixed economy. But a mixed economy in itself cannot be anything other than the fruit of a compromise and at the same time the arena of a struggle between various social forces.[55]

The experience of state entrepreneurship in the twentieth century shows that it is most effective when a need has appeared for assimilating new areas, for achieving new organizational and technological breakthroughs, and for creating the infrastructure and potential for further development. Capitalism was forced to reconcile itself to an advance by 'state socialism' in the 1950s and 1960s, because it had a need for this. The American economist Lester C. Thurow observes: 'Historically, private productivity growth and public infrastructure development are strongly correlated.'[56] Without public property the modern form of capitalism could simply not have developed. Globalization and liberalization became possible thanks to the preceding decades of economic expansion, which rested on the strength of the state economy.[57] The privatization in Eastern Europe became possible after the economic potential had been created by the state. Private capital came to the Internet only when the system had reached its maturity.

> In many cases to spread and accelerate economic development, infrastructure (transportation, communications, electrification) has to be built ahead of the market – but that means a long period of time before capitalistic profits are earned. Capitalists won't, and shouldn't, wait for those profits to appear. Capitalistic infrastructure can only be built behind, with or slightly ahead of the market. Historically, private money built America's railroads east of the Mississippi where markets already existed; public money was necessary to build them west of the Mississippi where the markets were to be built.

In such situations, profit simply cannot be the criterion: 'The issue is not the current payoffs from past infrastructure investments. Statistical studies of the past say nothing about whether new infrastructure should or should not be built. The Internet would have failed this test for twenty years.'[58]

The ability of the state sector to deliberately support loss-making enterprises for prolonged periods is not only its weak spot, but also its most important strategic advantage. The state sector creates a body of work without which rapid growth of the capitalist economy is impossible. The neo-liberal epoch is based on the achievements of the epoch of state entrepreneurship, including computer and space technology, infrastructure works, mass literacy and so forth. During the 1960s and 1970s even the governments which most consistently defended the principles of private initiative followed this path, justifying their actions on the basis of the need to concentrate resources for defence against communism. The 'communist myth' played a huge mobilizing role in the world economy; some built it while others fought against it, but both sides were forced to create new technologies and to transform society. After the state enterprise had done its work, however, the bourgeoisie no longer had any need for it. The bourgeoisie cannot develop new territories, but it is always ready to privatize anything that is built on them.

While making use of the body of work accumulated in the past, capitalist society is now failing to expand and renew it. In the words of Thurow, 'an era of shorter time horizons' is beginning.[59] The bases are thus being laid for a future crisis and for a new demand for state entrepreneurship.

The weakness of the state sector has always been its inability to carry forward its development on the basis of its own success. The state finds it easier to innovate than to administer. It finds it easier to create the new than to manage what has been created. This is why the state sector, after ensuring a breakthrough, loses the initiative and yields it to private enterprise. But does this mean that the state is doomed merely to plough the fields, the harvest from which will be gathered by private capital?

Transforming the State

It is clear that the model of the state enterprise, like the model of the state, needs to be dramatically altered. This is the essential task of radical reformism, the feature that distinguishes it from dogmatic currents of a communist or social democratic stripe. If the former are prepared to reproduce old institutions under the banners of 'workers' power' and 'people's property', the latter, referring to the failure of the former, increasingly reject any attempt at change.

The degree of readiness to nationalize strategically important sectors of the economy or monopoly enterprises can be taken as a measure of the seriousness of a reformist government. Both ruling elites and left-wing politicians know very well that even successful nationalization does not mean the destruction of capitalist relations in society. But it does create the possibility that qualitatively new institutions and a new relationship of social forces may appear. Nationalization limits the options for international finance capital. It is precisely the threat of property losses that forces the elites to make serious concessions. In other words, until the question of property is posed, smaller, 'individual' problems will not be solved.

The policy of nationalization pursued by the British Labour Party from 1945 to 1951 was extremely limited, but it created a favourable setting for a whole complex of social reforms. Meanwhile, the privatization, which by the early 1990s had become transformed into a global process, made all attempts to preserve the welfare state in East or West quite pointless.

Under the conditions of the crisis of socialism, the alternative to corporate capitalist entrepreneurship has ceased to be the state enterprise, but has become the spontaneously arising 'informal sector'. By the 1990s tens of millions of people throughout the world had been drawn into the informal sector. Property relations here are unclear and ambiguous, labour relations are regulated by personal agreements, and prices by the market in its old, pre-capitalist form. The informal sector allows the satisfaction of basic needs; it cannot give birth to massive economic growth or structural reforms. More and more, it is itself becoming the object of exploitation 'from outside', by big business. But its rise is a symptom of the fact that private capital is now unable to control the economic process.

Despite all the attacks, the idea of the state sector is gradually returning to the economic programmes of the left. The Labor Party of the United States, founded in 1996, does not once mention the word 'socialism' in its documents, but alongside pledges to fight for free education and universally accessible health care, these documents speak of the need to 'revitalize the public sector'.[60]

The environmental crisis demands changes in the approach taken to the use of resources. The cult of individual consumption, which has become a sort of motor of the world economy, is ruinous. However, a way out needs to be sought not in self-denial but in rational consumption. Wherever possible, individual consumption has to be replaced by collective consumption. This applies above all to transport, and to heating and utilities (water, gas, electricity). The basis for the effectiveness of collective consumption can only be high-quality socialized public services, under public control. The private sector, which is oriented toward profit, cannot solve this problem, and combining private initiative with municipal programmes always results in the hidden subsidizing of private business at the expense of society. Collective consumption presupposes municipal socialism, not only in the area of services but also in that of production.[61]

Forms and levels of socialization should be differentiated. Various types of production permit and demand different degrees of socialization. If the economy is complex, with a variety of different technological levels, the public sector can also only exist as a complex multi-level system, and not as the homogeneous, monolithic structure which socialists dreamed of in the past.

New Approach to Property

New technologies and new methods of organization also require changes in the approach taken to property. The American economist Wolfgang Streek, studying the work of Western firms trying to organize diversified quality production, discovered that most of them encountered the same problem, which he termed 'market and hierarchy failure'.[62] The combining of market criteria with hierarchy is a fundamental principle of management under capitalism. But in present-day conditions this principle fails to work, or prevents firms from establishing between themselves the new 'competition–cooperation' relations that are essential if technological potential is to be used to the full. 'New forms of governance', based on other approaches and values, are indispensable. We shall not find out from the works of the economists how to make these approaches and values the dominant ones in society.

The expanded role of pension funds, like the growth in the number of worker-owned enterprises and the vitality of the often-condemned state firm, prove that the traditional capitalist system of property has been exhausted to the point where it inevitably gives birth, in the course of its development, to various 'socialist' experiments. However, these 'buds of socialism' will not be able to transform society on their own. Even capitalism, which arose within feudal society, could not get by without massive expropriation of the property of the church and the aristocracy, or without the abolition of the feudal rights which served as the economic prop of the old classes. In just the same way, it is hard to imagine that the new society will manage to arise without violating capitalist concepts of the right of property.

Property is above all an expression of social relations. It is another question to what degree formal legal concepts succeed in expressing the essence of these relations. The Austrian jurist, Leo Specht, considers that leftists should not only criticize the concept of private property, but also ponder to what extent traditional concepts of property in general remain applicable. The task of the left consists of 'generating new legal relations, new forms of property, new forms of rights and obligations'. In Specht's view it is necessary to proceed both from the 'dualism of private and state-owned property' and from the counterposing of the collective enterprise to the nationalized one:

> Partnerships between the state (as general partner) and working collectives or members of working collectives can be designed. Such variations can depend on sectors of the economy, on the sources of finance, on the management know-how sometimes to be obtained from an outside party, on contributions of assets to the companies. Issues such as liability for the state-owned enterprises, the role of enterprises in contributing to the general well-being would influence the decision as to which porperty regime is to be applied. Yet the leading principle should be to restrict the choice of form and content of such property rights as little as possible.[63]

Specht's work was written using materials from Eastern Europe, but its conclusions have a more general significance, as does the whole economic experience of the former communist countries. It is quite obvious that future attempts at mechanically duplicating the Soviet model of centralized planning or of state enterprise are doomed to failure. But it is also obvious that a redistribution of power in the economy and society to the advantage of the majority, experimentation with property rights and radical changes in the position of workers on the job are all impossible without the state. If the state is deliberately stripped of the right to hold property, there cannot be any guarantees of property for workers, and no legally secure defence of the collective interests of the majority of the members of society. Nor can state regulation have any hope of success.[64]

State property is essential for attaining the strategic goals of the left. But after fulfilling its strategic tasks, state property cannot and must not be submerged in an administrative 'tactic'.

The functions of ownership have to be redistributed, not in favour of the private entrepreneurship that has now outlived its time, but of decentralized managerial structures that ensure the democratic participation of workers in decision-making. The forms of post-state management that are already familiar from the experience of the 1980s and 1990s include municipal and leasehold enterprises, independent collectives using public capital investments, and so forth. The globalization of the economy demands the creation of a new type of public enterprise, acting on the national level. Elements of this already exist. The intergovernmental programmes of the European Union have made it possible to create modern fighter aircraft, to launch satellites into space and to construct a tunnel under the English Channel. But in the conditions of capitalism the private sector will always reap the fruits of these labours.

The internationalization of the public sector is society's only real answer to the transnational corporations. The French economist Sylvian Hercberg notes in *Le Monde Diplomatique* that the idea of a democratically controlled all-European system of public services is already attracting notice and support. But this cannot be achieved unless the national state plays a key role.

> Coordination on a European level will become possible only as a result of common policies aimed at serving the general interest. If there is to be practical success, states must have the will to set up and to control, in selected sectors, structures that are aimed at carrying out the tasks of solidarity and equality, and that rest on the most modern technology.[65]

Advanced technology is becoming an area of struggle. For all its power, the private sector cannot exercise full control over technological developments. Consequently, the prospects for global socialization are real. 'If developed with international government sponsorship and cooperation', Nicholas Baran writes, 'the Internet could indeed become an international communications network, available to people of all nations, rich and poor alike.'[66] Public property can ensure the creation of generally accessible communications systems, answerable to users and under their control. But in the view of an American economist this scenario is improbable; it is not in the interests of the large corporations.

The source of exploitation is not machines and factory buildings that are in private hands, but capital. This was understood by Karl Marx in the nineteenth century, but still eludes the grasp of most theoreticians of self-management. Historically, Marxism called for the nationalization of the means of production to the degree that capital was embodied in them. A democratic economy is impossible without the socialization of the process of reproduction of capital – that is, of the processes of accumulation and investment.

When workers are drawn into participating in the ownership and management of property, does this represent an erosion of capitalist dominance, or is it merely a new technique of control and manipulation? It is in fact both, since on the one hand capitalism cannot get by without 'props' and 'social technologies' belonging to other epochs and social orders, while on the other hand, so long as the bourgeoisie holds power it will use even its own weakness to its advantage.

There is no one to represent the interests of the millions of people who are not part of the corporate elite. Until these masses of people take possession of the state and turn it into their instrument, everything will remain as it was. The traditional Marxist slogan of the abolition of private property remains timely. Without violating the principle of private property, it will be impossible either to create the society of which Marx and Engels dreamed, or to find a model of the mixed economy that is appropriate to the epoch. But for all this to happen, the state itself will have to be changed.

3
Nations and Nationalism

No one has ever managed to provide an exhaustive definition of a nation. Stalin, polemicizing in his time against the Austro-Marxists, listed a whole series of distinguishing characteristics. 'A nation is a stable, historically established community of people, which has arisen on the basis of a common language, territory, and economic and cultural life, and which has a common mentality manifesting itself in the field of culture.'[1] Stalin consciously excluded from his list of the characteristics of a nation the possession of its own state, since this would have led to 'justifying imperialist oppression' in relation to enslaved peoples.[2] It is obvious that by no means all nations are covered by this definition (in particular, Jews according to Stalin cannot constitute a nation). But the official Soviet Marxism-Leninism, right up until its demise in 1991, could not come up with anything better than Stalin's choice of distinguishing features.

The British scholar Benedict Anderson notes that the first modern national liberation movements were the revolts by the North American settlers and South American creoles against the colonial power of Britain and Spain. In neither case were the rebels any different from the colonizers in their ethnic origin, language or religion. Hence where nations are concerned, Anderson considers it possible to speak of 'imagined communities'.[3]

'Natural' Nations?

A nation is a historical and political phenomenon. Analysing the rise of new independent states on the territory of the former Soviet Union, the well-known Moscow commentator Dmitriy Furman has written: 'History is full of nations which for one reason or another did not come into being, and in our own age there are more than a few nations which, if history had turned out differently, if there had been a different "fall of the historical cards", might not have existed.'[4] Nations, like classes, are not 'natural'; they are born out of processes of political and economic development which include conscious work by political elites setting out to form their own 'national' culture.[5]

The creation of national states in Europe coincided with the rise of industrial capitalism and was organically linked to it. The transformation of communities and tribes into peoples, and of peoples into nations, occurred as an integral part of the process of formation of the modern state. 'A systematic look at the history of the modern world will show, I believe, that in almost every case statehood preceded nationhood, and not the other way round, despite a widespread myth to the contrary', argues Immanuel Wallerstein.[6]

The trouble is that in the process of modernization by no means all peoples have become nations. Meanwhile, states have arisen and collapsed, merged and split. Many peoples have developed within federations, at the same time possessing their statehood and not possessing it. Globalization, initiated by the centres of the world capitalist economy, has been superimposed on the continuing search for national self-identification and state self-organization in the countries of the periphery and semi-periphery. The incompleteness of this process helps explain the dramatic nature of the conflicts that have arisen in the late twentieth century.

It is in the nature of human beings to idealize movements that have achieved success. Bolshevism became a world-wide political model of revolutionary organization for sixty years because Lenin and Trotsky succeeded on 7 November 1917 in taking and holding on to power in Petrograd. National liberation movements have been idealized in the same way. Only later has it become evident that all national movements, even those which on the whole have adhered to leftist and democratic positions and have played a progressive role in history, have included reactionary components. Since the 1970s these reactionary tendencies in national movements have begun growing stronger, to a significant degree because of the growth of the general ideological and structural crisis of the left. In addition, the exhaustion of the democratic potential of traditional nationalism in a changed society is becoming more and more obvious.

It is obvious that attempts to solve traditional problems under qualitatively different social, cultural and technological conditions will have quite different consequences. The national state is not the same in the twentieth century as it was in the period from the seventeenth to the nineteenth centuries. But to create modern forms of statehood without passing through a period of historical ripening is impossible. This means an inevitable repetition of the bloody conflicts of the past, of the injustices, cruelties and authoritarian methods that lie at the basis of any state. It means the deliberate strengthening in society, even if only for a short time, of obsolete, archaic structures and relationships, the creation of new hierarchies clearly incompatible with the tasks of the modern world, and the implementation of policies which lag behind present-day life by a whole epoch. It is quite probable that the development of various peoples has been retarded and deformed because they have lacked their own states in the past. But the belated formation of a national state no longer compensates for this, just as gluttony in old age cannot make up for malnutrition in childhood. Moreover, the new state reflects all the contradictions and deformities of the earlier national development.

When a large number of countries revert simultaneously to barbarism, this cannot fail to make an impact on the rest of the world. From being a local, 'national' phenomenon, this regression becomes a global one. The need for national self-affirmation is quite real, and no less real are the catastrophic side-effects of this self-affirmation.

Civil wars and ethnic cleansing on the territory of the Yugoslav federation and the Soviet Union following their collapse are just as natural and inevitable in the process of forming new states as was, for example, the Franco-Prussian War in the history of Germany. New forms of oppression arise, along with new oppressed minorities (often, representatives of yesterday's 'imperial' nations). European public opinion, which clearly remembers the national injustices of the past, reacts very coldly to the complaints of the new minorities.

Typically, the new states on the territory of the former Soviet bloc did not arise where national oppression was strongest, but where the corresponding administrative units existed. The majority of Tatars remained outside the borders of Tatarstan, but when the leaders of the 'national movement' haggled with Moscow it was not over the rights of the Tatar population, but only over the status of the republic, where Russians made up no fewer than half of the inhabitants. Since the disintegration of the

Soviet Union a significant part of the Ukrainian population has remained in states such as Estonia or Kazakhstan, as part of the 'Russian-speaking community'. Their own state shows not the slightest interest in them.

Self-determination

Self-determination has been achieved not by peoples but by territories, and not by nations but by elites, by the bureaucratic apparatus. On becoming the new state power, the old bureaucracy tries to legitimize itself through aggressive national rhetoric and symbolic actions aimed at defending 'national interests' from the 'foreign adversary'. The worse the situation in the economy and social policy, the more important such activity becomes. The results include, for example, endless conflicts between Russia and Ukraine over Crimea and the Black Sea Fleet.

On the territory of the former USSR only two state formations have arisen which do not coincide with the old Soviet administrative entities: the Dnestr Moldavian Republic and the Chechen Republic, which has split not only from Russia, but also from Ingushetia, with which it was formerly united. It is significant that both of these states have remained unrecognized by the world community, and that military actions – albeit quite unsuccessful ones – have been launched against them. If Chechnya has won a certain sympathy (mainly due to the cruelty of the Russian occupation forces during the 1994–96 war), few people even within the former Soviet Union have shown interest in the Russian-speaking Dnestr Republic. Meanwhile, in these cases we really are dealing with a mass national movement arising 'from below'.

Western leftists are inclined to sympathize with 'small' peoples and to show no special liking for 'imperial' ones. They are ready to speak out against German, French, Russian, Serbian and with certain reservations, Croatian nationalism, while expressing sympathy for Ukrainian, Bosnian, Catalan and Quebecois nationalism. Meanwhile, they fail even to notice that 'small' nationalism usually becomes a real force when behind its back there looms the state interest of one or another of the 'large' 'imperialist' nations – the very same United States, Russia or Germany. Moreover, the bearers of the 'national idea' are most often not the oppressed masses, but the local bureaucracy.

In the 1980s and 1990s victories by nationalists in any region of the world have had a common geopolitical impact: they have strengthened the hegemony of the US as the sole world power. With the world economy becoming increasingly globalized, only large state formations are capable of pursuing autonomous financial and economic policies. In such circumstances it is quite obvious that world financial centres such as the International Monetary Fund and the World Bank, along with the ruling strata in the US, have an interest in combining increased economic integration with political disintegration. Collapsing federations and numerous small states, incapable of following an independent economic course, objectively require leadership from 'Big Brother'.

It is significant that, as in the case of the Soviet Union, most leftists have been unwilling not only to ponder the genuine meaning of their utterances on self-determination, but also to examine the class essence of each conflict or to consider how victory for the nationalists might affect the relationship of social and political forces in the world and in the region.

The 1995 referendum in Quebec was conducted by the Quebecois government very much in the spirit of the Soviet *nomenklatura*. The propaganda of the regional elite linked all the province's social and economic problems to the actions of the English-speaking 'centre'. As in the post-Soviet societies, the referendum question was formulated in a deliberately ambiguous manner. Instead of being asked for their views on the question of secession from Canada, the Quebecois were asked whether they wanted to give Quebec 'exclusive powers to pass its laws, levy all its taxes, and conclude all its treaties' in the framework of a 'new economic and political partnership' with Canada.[7] This ambiguous formulation, closely repeating the analogous formulations of post-Soviet *nomenklatura* referendums, allowed the government of Quebec to solve two problems at once. On the one hand, the formulation attracted the votes of many people who would not have voted for a split with Canada. On the other hand, the local authorities could interpret the results of the referendum as they wished. Whatever agreement they negotiated with the central government, from complete independence to autonomy in taxation matters, could be claimed as representing the will of the people. The local elites in Ukraine and Tatarstan followed precisely the same strategy. In 1992 residents of Kiev learned unexpectedly that they had voted not for a new union with Russia on an equal basis (as had been explained to them before the referendum), but for a break with Russia. The citizens of Tatarstan, thinking that they were voting for independence, found they had voted for tax autonomy.

What was in fact held in Quebec, as in the republics of the former USSR, was a referendum on expanding the powers of the regional elites. The difference between Canada and the Soviet Union lay in the fact that in Canada the effort to destroy the federation was unsuccessful. It was significant, however, that in Quebec and elsewhere a section of the left fully accepted and supported the nationalist demagogy of the regional elites.

The second referendum in Canada took place after the creation of the North American Free Trade Agreement (NAFTA). The success of the regional elites and the disintegration or weakening of Canada would have led only to a strengthening of the political, military and economic dominance of the US in the region.

'Imperial' and 'Non-historic' Peoples in Eastern Europe

Hostility to 'imperial' nations leads to a rejection of solidarity with members of the 'new minorities', even if they belong to the oppressed 'lower orders' of society. Complaints of oppression voiced by Russians or Serbs are not taken seriously, and neither is the question of the interests of the French in New Caledonia. When Russian nationalists or Le Pen in France divide the residents of their countries into indigenous and 'non-indigenous', this arouses the indignation of the progressive intelligentsia. When the anti-colonial movement or the government of the latest 'newly independent state' proposes to do the same, European left intellectuals find a multitude of reasons to justify this approach.

The democratic idea of equality of rights is offset, as it were, by the 'guilt complex' which representatives of the large nation are expected to experience. But the essence of the problem lies in the fact that every now and then the oppressed and oppressors change places. More than fifty years had to elapse after the fall of the Austro-Hungarian Empire before Europeans began to notice the existence of the Hungarian problem in Slovakia, Romania and Yugoslavia. Even in the 1970s a section of the Zionist movement tried to justify the oppression of Arabs in

Israel on the basis of the past sufferings of the Jewish people. It is unclear how much time will have to pass before someone in the West takes a serious attitude to the position of the Serbs and Russians who have become national minorities in the newly independent states. Meanwhile, in many cases they are deprived not only of their territorial but also of their cultural autonomy. During the Balkan War of the 1990s a substantial part of the Serbian population in Croatia stayed loyal to the government in Zagreb, hoping to receive equal citizenship rights in exchange. 'Although they are entitled by law and constitution to cultural autonomy, there are still no signs of such rights being provided', stated a London *War Report* in 1995.

> For example, Serbian children cannot learn their national script and language, or their literature and history. Serbs have a minimal presence in media organisations, and Serb life issues in Croatia are rarely covered. The Croatian government either prevents or manipulates the national and political organising of Serbs.[8]

Marx and Engels made the point that delayed realization of national hopes might be linked with social reaction. This is the essence of their concept of 'non-historic peoples'. In a book devoted to the views of Marx and Engels on the national question in Eastern Europe, the West Ukrainian socialist Roman Rosdolsky noted that they were mistaken in their assessment of the future of the western and southern Slavs, identifying progress and modernization with their Germanization. At the same time, Rosdolsky says:

> though Engels was immoderate in his praise of the consequences of the historical process and greatly exaggerated their significance in the case of the Slavs, this was not because he wanted to call a halt to the evolution of society, but because he wanted to propel it forward. In his own impetuous way he believed that these consequences anticipated what he regarded as the next task of history – the abolition of all 'particularism', the fusing of Europe's population into ever greater political and economic units.[9]

'Non-historic peoples' suppressed the revolution in Austro-Hungary; Croatians, Romanians, Slovaks, Serbs and Ukrainians were all used by the empire against the Austrian and Hungarian democrats. Marx and Engels made a contradictory assessment of the Czechs, to whom it was impossible to deny the status of a historic nation. Only Poland was regarded by the founders of Marxism as a fully historic nation, deserving support in its struggle for independence. Whatever attitude we might now take to Engels's views, the role played by the western Slavs in the events of 1848 was not a matter of chance. Nor was there anything accidental about the powerful rise of nationalist reaction in Eastern Europe following the collapse of Austro-Hungary in 1918 and after the fall of the Communist bloc in 1989.

In 1918 most of the 'non-historic' peoples managed to establish their own states, but with the exception of Czechoslovakia (where the 'non-historic' Slovak nation was subordinated to the 'historic' Czechs), none of these states was democratic. The creation of new states was everywhere accompanied by the oppression of national minorities, by repression, by the crushing of the workers' movement, and by cultural isolationism and provincialism. The second wave of national renewal, that began after 1989, is to a significant degree duplicating the first, with the difference that ethnic cleansing in the former Yugoslavia has taken on a more massive and appalling character. One should not forget that ethnic cleansing took place earlier in this region. It is enough to recall the fascist regimes that were set up in Croatia and Slovakia in the period from 1939 to 1941 with the help of Nazi Germany, or the actions of Ukrainian, Hungarian and Romanian fascists in the occupied territories of the Soviet Union. These same peoples provided heroic examples of anti-fascist resistance. But this was not only resistance to the German forces, but also a struggle against their own nationalist reaction and home-grown fascism. So it was in the course of the Slovakian national uprising, and also in the case of the partisan struggle waged in Yugoslavia under the leadership of Josip Broz Tito.

Following the victory over fascism in 1945 and the installing of the communist regimes in 1947 and 1948, ethnic cleansing did not come to an end. Germans were expelled from the provinces ceded to Poland, and Germans and Hungarians from the border regions of Czechoslovakia. Later, a significant part of the Jewish population that survived the Nazi occupation was forced to leave Poland. The position of the Hungarians who remained in Transylvania, which had again passed to Romania, was burdensome.

On the territory of the Soviet Union the formation of new independent states was also accompanied not only by armed conflicts, but also by reprisals against peaceful residents. While the actions of the Serbian forces in Bosnia were condemned by the world community as war crimes, the world appeared not to notice the analogous events that occurred during the Armenian–Azerbaijani and Georgian–Abkhazian conflicts.

Summing up the results of national policy in the republics of the former Soviet Union, the Russian Marxist Aleksandr Tarasov wrote that it was the national idea that had allowed the old and new elites to keep peoples in subjection following the collapse of the old system of control.

> But the games of 'national rebirth' and of national exclusivity are not ending up well. 'The voice of the blood' demands blood. The horrors of Sumgait, Karabakh, Osh and Fergana have allowed us to see with our own eyes what was clear long ago from theory: that the demon of nationalism requires bloody sacrifices. The 'national idea' has its own internal logic of development. It moves rightward, in the direction of fascism (whatever name is ultimately applied to it), until blood begins to flow, and then will not be sated. Those who want to climb on board this idea will be forced to travel with it.[10]

The idea of national statehood is linked closely with violence. A nation which no one threatens does not have an acute need for its own national state. A modern state cannot be reduced to organized violence. Nevertheless, organized violence is in historical terms the first principle of the formation of states. It plays a huge role in the creation of national self-consciousness. It is not by chance that monuments to military leaders adorn the squares of most European cities, including the most peaceful. Liberation wars help to create a military power which is then often used for aggression. Most defensive wars have finished up with the making of conquests. Any soldier knows that wars are in general impossible to win if one is restricted solely to defence. If there is even the slightest possibility of pursuing retreating aggressors to their own territory, an effort is made to do this.

International conflict also gives birth to such ideas, fully justified from the point of view of the national interest, as 'secure borders', 'the struggle for an exit to the sea' and so forth. While defending its right to create an independent state, Germany seized Alsace and Lorraine from France. Later, the Polish struggle against German aggression led to the annexation to Poland of Germany's eastern provinces. The struggle by Israel for survival and secure frontiers ended with its occupying Arab lands for many years. The example of Russia from the sixteenth to the eighteenth century is especially revealing. Cut off from the sea, effectively blockaded by its Western neighbours and constantly subject to attacks from Poland and Sweden, the country was unable to modernize itself and maintain its independence without an exit to the sea. Successive rulers saw in this their historic mission. Peter the Great, at his second attempt, managed to take Narva from the Swedes, and also to capture Tallinn and Riga. Catherine the Great seized the Crimea. Russia became a fully-fledged European power.

The same history seems quite different if we relate it from the point of view of the Estonians, Latvians or Crimean Tatars. It is not surprising that little Estonia, which became independent in 1918, soon tried to shift its border beyond Narva. Weakened by the Civil War, Russia in 1920 signed the Peace of Tartu, as a result of which Estonia gained the historically Russian town of Ivangorod, built in the middle ages by the rulers of Novgorod for the purpose of defence against German attacks coming from the direction of the same Narva. After Estonia regained its independence in 1991, the Estonian government made constant claims on Ivangorod, citing the Peace of Tartu. In Tallinn maps were printed in which parts of the territory of Russia were shown as Estonian, and a depiction of Ivangorod Castle appeared on Estonian crowns.

As Wallerstein notes, the oppression of minorities is at times due not to prejudices on the part of the dominant nationality, but to the demands of bureaucratic rationality. 'States. . . have an interest in administrative uniformity that increases the efficacy of their policies. Nationalism is the expression, the promoter and the consequence of such state-level uniformities.'[11] In other words, Estonian or Ukrainian functionaries who force Russians to submit documents exclusively in the 'state language' (which some of these officials themselves speak only with difficulty) do this not from hostility to the former 'imperial nation', but simply for the sake of convenience and in order to standardize record-keeping.

The destruction of the eastern European federations was viewed by many leftists as a continuation of the national liberation struggle of the colonial countries. Almost no one paid any attention to a fundamental difference that made such comparisons impossible. The anti-colonial uprisings, from the time of the American war of independence, were simultaneously struggles both for civil rights and for economic self-determination. The inhabitants of the colonies rose up against a situation in which the main decisions concerning their lives were taken by European parliaments and governments which they had not elected. If the British crown had made a timely decision to grant the American colonists places at Westminster, today's world political map might look quite different.

The inhabitants of the eastern European federations, by contrast, were citizens of their states, with equal rights. This was not merely formal. For some reason no one on the western left has cared to examine the role which the Russian, Czech or Serbian elites played in the destruction of the various federal states. From the point of view of imperial logic, these elites might have been expected to hold out for the preservation of unity. But what happened was the opposite. It was Moscow that insisted on the dissolution of the USSR despite resistance from the republics of Central Asia, dissatisfaction in Belarus and an ambiguous situation in Ukraine. It was from Prague, and not from Bratislava, that the initiative came for dividing Czechoslovakia into two states. Later, all efforts by Belarus to reunite with Russia came up against a wall of incomprehension in Moscow. And was it not the Serbian nationalism of Slobodan Milosevic that played a tragic role in destroying Yugoslav unity in the early 1990s?

The Russian elite knew perfectly well that the economic life of the separate republics would, as before, be determined by decisions taken in Moscow. But earlier, the republics themselves had enjoyed the possibility of influencing these decisions through the institutions of the federation. Now they had lost this possibility. But if the independence of the new states was very limited, Moscow's ability to control the processes unfolding there also turned out to be much less than might have been expected.

Where the former federal centre lost control on the periphery, the vacuum was quickly filled by the West.

In supporting nationalist movements, left activists have preferred not to think about these movements' social bases. Not only do such movements rest on petty bourgeois elements and on state officialdom, but they are also in conflict with a significant part of the working class that belongs to the 'non-indigenous nation'.

On this level, the language policy of modern-day nationalism is extremely suggestive. Analysing the rise of national consciousness in Finland, the historian Risto Alapuro stresses that the efforts of nationalists in the late nineteenth century to restrict the use of the Swedish language and to replace it with Finnish were closely linked with the policy 'of creating an upper class, culturally united with the majority of the people, largely by linguistic conversion'.[12] The same could be said of the Czech or Baltic nationalism of the same epoch. In societies where the traditional ruling classes preferred a 'foreign' language, calls for a return to the language of the people had a clear democratic thrust. But everything is quite different in present-day societies where it is immigrant working people – the most oppressed sector of society – who speak the 'foreign' language, while the elites are defending their privileged position, among other ways by erecting a linguistic barrier. Within this scheme the 'national' language often fulfils the same social function in the late twentieth century as the 'foreign' language in nineteenth-century society.

For leftists, the price of refusing to address such 'trifles' has been moral bankruptcy, disorientation, and the loss of the left's social base. The desire to present all opponents of regional nationalism as reactionaries causes many radical writers to close their eyes to obvious facts. In Britain, for example, a significant part of the left press stubbornly denies the very existence of a working class in the Protestant community of Northern Ireland, or equates any positive reference to the rights of the Protestant community with a call for maintaining the power of London over the six counties.

The unselfish love shown by leftists for nationalist movements fighting against 'imperialist domination' has not always been reciprocated. Discussing the differences between the approaches taken by leftists and nationalists, the outstanding British historian Eric Hobsbawm notes that the cause of the Irish Republican Army has aroused sympathy among British leftists despite sharply different views on questions of values, goals and tactics.

> For the Left, Ireland was, historically, one, but only one, out of the many exploited, oppressed and victimized sets of human beings for which it fought. For the IRA kind of nationalism, the Left was, and is, only one possible ally in the fight for its objectives in certain situations. In others it was ready to bid for the support of Hitler as some of its leaders did during World War II.[13]

Marx and Engels were absolutely right when they declared that no people can be free while it oppresses other people. But they were talking specifically about oppression; the existence of multinational states did not in itself strike them as unnatural. Engels at the end of his life even expressed the hope that it might prove possible to transform the British Empire into a democratic multinational community. In Britain, the 'Irish question' was a highly contentious issue during the nineteenth century, and in a different form it remains so to this day. But the 'Scottish question' was not on the agenda of nineteenth-century British politics, although the union of Scotland with England had been effected and consolidated in the face of stubborn resistance that lasted for centuries. The reason why this question ceased to be contentious was simple – as the British imperial system took shape, the Scottish Protestant majority quickly became integrated into it, while Catholic Ireland remained an oppressed periphery.

'National Question' or the Problem of Democracy?

The struggle against all forms of national oppression is an obligatory part of any consistent democratic programme. However, the creation of an independent state cannot be seen as the only possible answer to the question. Since Marxists first rejected Marx's view that the assimilation of non-historic peoples was desirable and progressive, socialist thinkers have advanced three alternatives for solving the national question: federalism, 'self-determination up to the point of secession' and cultural-national autonomy.

Expressing their solidarity with the century-and-a-half-long struggle of the Poles for independence from Russian tsarism, the Russian social democrats spoke of the right of nations to self-determination. Meanwhile, their comrades in Austria were inclined to see a serious problem here. For the Austro-Marxists the national question was above all cultural, not political. Religious freedom, equal language rights and cultural-national autonomy within the framework of a single state would in their view solve the problem. To Lenin and the Russian Bolsheviks, such an approach seemed opportunist. Autonomy and rights were meaningless unless they were reflected in the realm of power.

Subsequent experience has shown that this is not always so. Aside from the fact that questions of culture and power are linked much more closely than might seem at first glance, cultural-national autonomy can also have administrative and hence political consequences. It may coincide with regional autonomy in areas where a particular 'minority' makes up the 'majority' or at least a substantial sector of the population. This is how the national problem of the Swedish minority in Finland was resolved. Meanwhile in Switzerland, divided into cantons, the problem does not exist at all.

Criticizing the Austro-Marxists, Lenin noted the ambiguity of the idea of 'national liberation'. He set out to reveal the social basis of the conflict.

> Inasmuch as the bourgeoisie of the oppressed nation struggles against the oppressors we are always, in every instance, its most determined supporters, since we are the boldest and most determined enemies of oppression. Inasmuch as the bourgeoisie of the oppressed nation defends its own bourgeois nationalism, we are its opponents.[14]

This position allowed Lenin to support the liberation movements in Poland and Finland in the period before 1917, and in the years from 1920 to 1922 to call for the occupation of Georgia and Armenia by Soviet forces. From Lenin's point of view there was no contradiction here. What was involved in the first case was a struggle by the oppressed bourgeoisie against tsarism, and in the second, a struggle by bourgeois nationalists against a proletarian revolution. The problem was that contrary to Lenin's view, nationalism does not arise only in a bourgeois milieu.

Perhaps more strongly than anywhere else, the nationalism of the twentieth century has developed in the middle classes, in the bureaucratic milieu and among representatives of the 'free professions' for whom 'ethnicity' and a sense of participation in 'their culture' have been able to provide guarantees of earnings, career advancement and independence. Hence the 'anti-bourgeois essence' of the national struggle in no way provides a guarantee that it will be democratic or leftist.

In the controversies of the early years of the century Rosa Luxemburg took an independent position. 'For Rosa Luxemburg, national independence was a bourgeois fetish on a par with the "women's rights" she mocked with equal vehemence', notes her biographer R. Abraham.[15] Luxemburg's position might seem to have been the most consistent and uncontradictory in these debates. For her, both the Bolsheviks and the Austro-Marxists were to an equal degree hostages of petty-bourgeois nationalism. But in practice, everything was more complex.

> As the Russian Civil War ground on, Bolshevik acceptance of 'self-determination of nations' undermined the Russian Whites in the borderlands of the former Empire. . . . Even more important, it committed the socialist revolution internationally to alliance with national liberation struggles by non-European peoples against European imperialism, while remaining free to rally national resistance to fascism during the Second World War. Pressed to a conclusion that she was anxious to avoid, Rosa Luxemburg's views, if adopted by socialists everywhere, would have given international socialism the choice between a de facto alliance with imperialism or neutrality in many of the crucial struggles of the twentieth century.[16]

The only concept which Marxists in the period before the First World War failed to think through definitively was therefore that of federalism, which remained the exclusive 'intellectual property' of anarchists and of 'petty bourgeois' radical democrats. It was only during the Civil War that Lenin 'discovered' federalism as a way of solving the national question. The results of the First World War included not only the disintegration of the empires in Central and Eastern Europe, but also the rise of the multinational Soviet federation. The subsequent transformation of Yugoslavia and Czechoslovakia into federations should in theory have confirmed the correctness of this approach. The federative principle presupposed establishing quasi-statehood for each nationality, while at the same time retaining a 'common homeland'. Such homelands were defended by Yugoslav partisans, by Slovak insurgents and by the multinational Soviet Army in the struggle against Nazi occupiers who tried to set up puppet national states in Croatia and Slovakia, and later in Belarus as well.

The events of the late twentieth century are forcing us to rethink the past. Loyalty to the 'common homeland' has grown significantly weaker in the epoch of global consumer society. In the absence of a unifying ideology, multinational federations fell apart after 1989 just like former empires.

Returning to the Old Debates

So who was right in the discussions of the early twentieth century? With hindsight, scholars find themselves in the position of the rabbi in the Jewish joke who tells each of the participants in an argument, 'You're right!' To his wife's objection that both sides cannot be right, the rabbi answers, 'And you, wife, are right as well!'

In reality, the debates of that period merely showed that not only is there is no single answer to the national question, but there is no single national question either. The parties were in essence talking about different things. Lenin's position reflected the reality of the Russian Empire, where the various national regions had more or less homogeneous populations, while the position of his opponents reflected the situation in Central Europe, with its mixed population. It is one of the ironies of history that after the Peace of Versailles it was Lenin's concept of self-determination that was finally implemented in Central Europe, while the Soviet Union was built on a combination of federalism and cultural-national autonomy in the spirit of Bauer.

The weak point of Lenin's concept of 'self-determination' is the stress it places on the administrative-political status of a particular territory. What is the crucial element here – the people or the land? In principle, self-determination, according to Lenin, cannot be separated from a definite territorial area. For this reason it is not only prone to infringe upon the rights of minorities inhabiting the same territory, but it also limits the realization of the national rights of that section of the people that lives outside the territory's boundaries. Tatars, for example, have enjoyed a range of advantages in Tatarstan, which since 1991 has been a semi-independent state within the Russian Federation. But no one, including the government of Tatarstan, has shown much concern for the national and cultural rights of the great majority of Tatars, who live outside the 'self-determined' territory. In a certain sense their position has become worse. In analogous fashion the self-determination of Ukraine has harmed the interests of millions of Ukrainians living in Russia, Kazakhstan and other former Soviet republics, where they have begun to be assimilated rapidly into the 'Russian-speaking community'. In fairness, it should be noted that for all the outrages suffered by representatives of Russian culture in the newly independent states, the position of cultural minorities in the 'new Russia' is even worse.

In many cases a national ideology has arisen out of rivalry between elites struggling to divide up the 'right' to oppress one and the same people. That is not to say that the idea of self-deter-mination lacks democratic potential; the exercising of self-determination normally presupposes freedom of choice and democratic decision-making. But, in practice, everything is likely to happen differently. Often, self-determination is exercised not by the population but by the government, acting in the name of an abstract, metaphysical nation.

Where self-determination opens the way for people to win rights and freedoms they had been denied in an 'alien' state, this is a huge step forward. The demand for self-determination may be spurred not only by national oppression, but also by the undemocratic character of the 'common' state – this was the case with the rise of nationalism in Eastern Europe and the Soviet Union. The first free elections in the entire history of Chechnya took place there only after the expulsion of the Russian Army in 1996. Decolonization was a boon for the peoples it affected only to the degree that it opened up for them the path to an independent civil existence. But many of the conquests of the period of anti-colonial struggle were wrested from these peoples by their own victorious 'national' elites. The same thing is happening on the territory of the former Soviet Union. On the level of civil rights, many of the former Soviet republics took a huge step backward between 1991 and 1996 even by comparison with the far-from-democratic Soviet period. It is not surprising that nostalgia for the USSR had begun to appear by the mid-1990s not only in Russia, but also in other 'newly independent states'.

The assumption that the free development of a nation is possible only on the basis of its own statehood is not borne out by history. In exactly the same way, there are no grounds for believing that only members of the dominant nationality can be loyal citizens of the state.

It can readily be seen, for example, that ethnic nationalism in the Baltic republics has not had the effect of consolidating their independent statehood, but of weakening it. Depriving a significant part of their inhabitants of civil rights, Estonia and Latvia have created for themselves a difficult domestic and international political problem that does not exist in neighbouring Lithuania. The segregation, however, has also had other causes that have nothing to do with nationalist ideology. In Latvia and Estonia, where the bulk of the Russian-speaking population have been officially deprived of civil rights, it is obvious that this discrimination is more social than national. By 1989 the Russian-speaking community was only very weakly represented within the bureaucracy and within the intellectual and commercial elites, at the same time as it made up the overwhelming majority of the working class. Most Russian-speaking members of the elite had either obtained citizenship or left the republic. In Lithuania, where the social divide does not coincide with the ethnic one, and where members of the Lithuanian community make up the bulk of the working class, no one has even tried to deprive immigrants of their civil rights.

The emergence of a Russian-speaking bourgeoisie that had grown rich on trade with the former metropolis changed the situation dramatically, making the earlier discriminatory measures largely pointless. Servicing Russian transit trade has accounted for about a fifth of Latvia's Gross Domestic Product in the 1990s, and between 70 and 90 per cent of the people employed in this sector are 'non-citizens'. They have set up a total of 1,190 joint enterprises with Russian firms. 'Non-citizens are doing the most business with Russia', reported the newspaper the *Baltic Times*, adding that it is the Russian community that suffers most from the various sanctions against

Latvia introduced by Moscow on the pretext of defending the Russian population.[17]

'Before our eyes', notes *Nezavisimaya gazeta*, 'Russians in Latvia and Estonia, who are excluded from legal politics, have quickly come to occupy key positions in business, just like Jews in medieval Europe. Their "national character" has not been an impediment.'[18] Of course, only an insignificant minority of the Russian-speaking community have achieved success in business. But this has been enough to make their integration essential; establishing a bourgeois national state requires a united elite, not one divided along ethnic lines. In exactly the same way, the rise of an entrepreneurial class among the black majority in South Africa forced the white bourgeoisie to make the transition to more liberal, less racist positions. The concept of nationhood underwent a rethinking; ethnic or racial principles were replaced by affiliation with a particular state.

History provides a number of examples in which minorities have identified themselves strongly with 'alien' states. These minorities include the Finnish Swedes, who stress proudly that they are different from the 'royal Swedes' in Stockholm; the Alsace Germans, for whom the French Revolution became a fundamentally important part of their own history; and the French and Italian-speaking Swiss. It is significant that all these groups border on 'kindred' states that are relatively strong and influential. But not only are the minorities uninterested in uniting with these states; if necessary, they are even prepared to defend themselves against claims from these quarters. Historically, this is explained by the fact that as minorities in 'alien' states all these groups have enjoyed no fewer, and at times even more civil and cultural rights than they would have received in their 'own' states. 'Sempre liberi, sempre svizzeri!' proclaimed the inhabitants of the Italian regions of Switzerland – forever free, and forever Swiss. The border defended them from the feudal oppression, plunder and raids that laid waste to neighbouring Italy. The Swedish minority in Finland, comprising less than a tenth of the population, makes up an important part of the national elite and enjoys cultural and national autonomy. The Swedish language, which most people in Finland do not understand, has equal status with Finnish as an official language. It is curious that the situation of the French-Canadians in Quebec is in many ways similar. The difference, however, lies in the fact that the Swedish bourgeoisie and intelligentsia in Finland make up the most open and cosmopolitan sector of society, while in Quebec the francophone bourgeoisie is distinguished by its provincialism.

The cases in which minorities have been successfully integrated show that the national question is ultimately one of civil and cultural rights. Where these rights are violated, nationalism is transformed from the ideology of narrow ethnic and corporative groups into a mass movement. In this respect, the Armenians, Chechens and Kurds provide typical examples. These peoples have continually been subject to repression, forced resettlement and genocide. Not surprisingly, they have come to see the creation of their own state as a sort of guarantee of survival. Nevertheless, even among representatives of the Kurdish national movement there is an understanding of the fact that having their own state would not solve the problems of most Kurds. Abdullah Ochelan, the leader of the Kurdistan Workers Party (PKK), which since 1984 has been waging a guerrilla war against the Turkish army, declared in March 1994: 'Contrary to the widespread belief in Turkey, I am not convinced that secession from Turkey is the best solution for the Kurds, not even when we have the military strength to achieve this.' He added, 'A landlocked country, surrounded by enemies in all four directions, is the worst solution for Kurdish independence. Even if Turkey secedes from the Kurds, we will not let you go.'[19] Shamil Basaev, the Chechen insurgent leader, famous for his heroic and unbending defence of independence, in 1996 stressed that his people needed 'concord' with Russia:

> I appreciate that if we load the republic onto our backs like a sack, we will not be able to go anywhere. As the saying is, 'not in Russia, but with Russia'. We are content to live in the same building, but only in our own apartment.[20]

It would be very dangerous to idealize Chechen nationalism, but the actual conditions under which it developed should not be forgotten. Leftists sympathized with the Chechen insurgents not out of support for the idea of an independent Chechnya, but because the Chechen struggle undermined the Yeltsin regime and hastened the process of change in Russia. In exactly the same fashion, Lenin and other 'defeatists' spoke out against the

military operations of the tsarist government not because they
wanted victory for German imperialism, but because they
understood that failure in the war would lead to revolution and
to the liberation of Russia. Meanwhile, the ruling layers in the
US and Western Europe gave support in practice to the aggression
against the Chechen people. They abolished the limitations,
imposed under international agreements signed by the Soviet
government, on the concentration of armed forces in Russia's
southern regions, and provided additional loans to Moscow
when the Russian budget began to collapse under the weight of
military spending.

The repression to which the Kurds and Chechens were
subjected, like the Armenians and Jews in earlier times,
convinced them that they had no choice but to create their own
army, their own government and their own laws. But the
authority of this government would still be limited to a particular
territory. Meanwhile, as a direct result of the repression, major
sections of these peoples finished up scattered about 'foreign'
territories. This was the case with the Jews and Armenians, and
later with the Kurds and Chechens. In the case of the Jews and
Armenians the population was dispersed not only about the
regions of the former empire, but throughout the world; this is
now true of the Kurds as well. Not even the existence of an
independent state is enough to provide guarantees to all the
members of a nationality in such circumstances.

The guerrilla war waged by the PKK in Turkish Kurdistan has
forced most of the Kurdish peasants from mountain regions to
become urban workers in Istanbul, Izmir and Ankara, or even in
the industrial centres of western Germany. One of the ideologues
of the Turkish left, Ertugrul Kurkcu, has noted that however
events transpire an inevitable result will be:

> coexistence between Kurds and Turks within the present
> boundaries of the Turkish Republic. This requires a labour-
> oriented political path appealing to the workers, urban poor
> and intellectuals of both Turkish and Kurdish origin, as well
> as to other nationalities living in the country.

This means that the requirements for success include not just
nationalism, even if this is 'revolutionary', but 'modern labour
politics'.[21] The researcher of the Kurdish national movement,

Abbas Vali, stresses that the Kurdish problem cannot be solved without radical democratic changes in the states to which this oppressed people are now subject:

> Crucially, the introduction of a democratic conception of citizenship would serve not only to guarantee individual rights and obligations. It would also define all the ethnic, racial and religious conditions for membership in the states and societies of Iran, Iraq, Turkey and Syria. The introduction of such a non-ethnic, non-racial, non-religious conception of citizenship should be the objective of all political efforts to resolve the Kurdish question by respecting Kurdish identity and ensuring its civil and political expressions within a democratic and constitutional framework.[22]

National Liberation and Capitalism

The approach taken by the left to the national question has traditionally been part of a general anti-capitalist strategy. After the Russian Revolution and the end of the First World War the discussion between the Austro-Marxists, Lenin and Rosa Luxemburg became part of history. Once in power, the Bolsheviks were forced to abandon many of their initial theoretical positions and to improvise. So long as the war in Europe continued, their key slogan was 'for a peace without annexations or indemnities'. After the hopes of revolution in Germany had collapsed, the Russian revolutionaries placed increasing hopes on the colonial peoples. Until 1918 the 'colonial question' had not held a particularly important place in socialist ideology. Now a rise in anti-colonial nationalism became an essential element in the general strategy for breaking the chain of capitalism 'at its weak link'. Nevertheless, the support given by the Communist Parties to the anti-colonial struggle was not unconditional. The communists of the 1920s and 1930s were still able to distinguish reactionary from progressive nationalism. Also, the anti-colonial movements did not always have the same priorities as the workers' movements in industrialized countries. This was especially apparent during the years of the struggle against fascism, when many representatives of Arab nationalism placed their hopes on Nazi Germany as a potential source of support in their struggle for liberation from Britain. The Communist International did not support the Quit India Movement in 1942, since the actions of Indian nationalists were preventing the British Empire from concentrating its strength on the struggle against fascism (and from fulfilling its obligations as an ally of the USSR).

During the years of the Second World War anti-colonial rhetoric virtually disappeared from the utterances of communist and social democratic leaders. However, traces of it were to be found in speeches by political leaders in the US. Naturally, the anti-colonialism of the Democratic administration in Washington was not without self-interest; amid the weakening of the British Empire and the effective collapse of the French colonial system the US for the first time had an opportunity to transform itself from the economic into the military and political leader of the West, filling the vacuum that had arisen.

A new wave of anti-colonialism on the left took place in the 1950s and 1960s. On the one hand the communist movement, as it grew accustomed to the 'Cold War' between East and West, returned to the concept of the 'weak link'. On the other, the incipient new left movement saw in the colonial revolutions hope for the appearance of a new socialist model, distinct from Stalinist totalitarianism. The revolutions in China, Vietnam and Cuba heightened this mood. The struggle against American intervention in Vietnam acted as a mobilizing factor for a new wave of anti-capitalist opposition in Western countries themselves. The slogan 'Thirty new Vietnams!' sounded convincing.

A further process was also apparent. If the anti-colonial movements of the 1920s had often been traditionalist and even reactionary, headed by torpid feudal elites, after the Second World War and the proclaiming of Indian independence the situation changed. In colonial and semi-colonial countries where a native industrial proletariat, a bureaucracy and an educated middle class had arisen, interest in socialism was growing. A progressive and democratic nationalism that had first appeared in India (to some degree under the influence of British political culture) first spread to other dependent countries and was then forced onto the sidelines by more radical concepts of liberation. The combination of left ideology, borrowed from Western Europe and the Soviet Union, with home-grown nationalist aspirations gave rise to the national liberation movements of the 1960s and 1970s. Decolonization and the new, sometimes merely simulated revolutions, fed the romantic anti-imperialism of Western leftists.[23] No one regarded the concept of the 'national question' as a 'weak point' of Marxism, and in essence the question itself did not exist; there was only imperialism and the anti-colonial struggle of the peoples.

The situation changed radically in the 1980s. The West seized the initiative and began to use nationalist movements in the struggle against communism. New insurgencies appeared, armed by the US Central Intelligence Agency. The Afghan *mujaheddin* were also fighting for independence, but this time against Soviet forces and their allies. The situation was even more confused because many slogans of the anti-communist resistance were precisely the same as those of the earlier national liberation movement. National dissatisfaction was also becoming more obvious in the countries of Eastern Europe and in the USSR itself. The weaker the democratic and socialist alternative, the more attractive nationalism appeared.

Meanwhile, the victorious national liberation movements were turning to the right. The shift by Egypt in the 1970s still seemed an exception, but it soon became clear that this was in fact a general rule. Once the national bureaucracy had taken power, it did not need a continuation of revolution, but stability, investment, and recognition from Western elites. The weaker the Soviet Union, the more quickly the reorientation proceeded, but the decisive reasons for the turn were not foreign but domestic.

Then at last came the year 1989, when the communist system disintegrated and the left movement in Europe suffered an unmistakable moral collapse. Globalization and neo-liberalism meant that the old anti-imperialist and anti-colonial slogans became empty; the hegemony of the 'centre' was now being exercised through new methods. But radicals continued mechanically to repeat the old formulas that everyone had grown sick of hearing.

During the 1960s and 1970s solidarity with Vietnam or with the peoples of Latin America had been a mobilizing factor for the left movement, especially in the United States. It had helped the movement recruit new members and to express its distinctive identity. With the 1990s everything changed. For disillusioned radicals, solidarity became a profession. New activists were not recruited, and fundraising became oriented increasingly toward supporting one's own little group.

From the anti-imperialist romanticism, the rhetoric and a general 'anti-imperial mood' remained, but no one could formulate a clear, positive programme. Myths and simplified interpretations were cultivated, in the spirit of the American cinema with its good guys and bad guys. Yesterday's Arab or Yugoslav 'heroes' became villains, while more and more often the US Marines were perceived not as the armed vanguard of Western capital, but as a neutral force called in to restore justice.

Bombs and Multiculturalism

The intellectual crisis of the Western left made itself felt with horrifying acuteness during the war in Bosnia. During the days when American and British aircraft were hammering Serbian positions, *Socialist Campaign Group News*, the organ of left-wing Labour members of the British parliament, published two appeals in a single issue. One, signed by Labour Friends of Bosnia, called on readers to support 'the use of comprehensive air strikes'. This, it was argued, should be followed by more forceful military intervention in order to help the Sarajevo government in Bosnia, which was attempting 'to recreate a multi-ethnic, open, plural and democratic political community'. Counterposed to this was an appeal from the Committee for Peace in the Balkans. Stating that all sides in the conflict had committed atrocities, this accused the West and NATO of having double standards. No one, it said, had condemned the expulsion of hundreds of thousands of Serbs from Krajina by the Croats, or the destruction by the Bosnian army of 200 Serbian villages in the Srebrenica region. 'To add the atrocity of NATO bombing to those already taking place will contribute nothing to the cause of peace in the former Yugoslavia's civil war.'[24]

Western leftists obviously lacked clear criteria for assessing what was going on. Most of them initially supported the disintegration of Yugoslavia in the name of national self-determination, then rejected the right to self-determination of Serbs (and to some degree Croats) in the name of a united, multinational, multicultural Bosnia. The problem was that the democratic, multicultural Bosnia was a myth from the very beginning. The collapse of Yugoslavia had made retaining Yugoslav cultural pluralism in a single republic an obvious impossibility.

The Bosnian authorities were not 'Islamic fundamentalists', as the pro-Serbian mass media in Russia argued. But neither were they democrats or supporters of cultural pluralism. They were nationalists and pragmatists. When talking to the West they stressed their pluralism; when talking to Arab sponsors they spoke of their fidelity to Islam; and at home they followed policies aimed at consolidating their own authoritarian state.

Labour Focus on Eastern Europe, which took a thoroughly hostile attitude to the Serbs, acknowledged: 'The new Bosnian government, with its Muslim majority, was not regarded by the Serb or Croat population as "their" government. The government acted as a Muslim government, with very dubious language about a Muslim state.'[25] While the Sarajevo leaders were calling for Western intervention in the name of defending cultural pluralism, the domestic policies of this administration had little in common with such principles. The Sarajevo regime 'made no attempt to mobilise the population, to build on and strengthen the practice of living together, to appeal to the defenders of multi-ethnic society in Croatia and Serbia'.[26]

The myth of model democrats from the Bosnian government in Sarajevo, defending the country from Serbian totalitarian villains, does not stand up to examination either. This is not because the Serbian leaders in Bosnia and Yugoslavia were good in themselves, but simply because their Bosnian and Croatian adversaries were in practice no better.

The Party for Democratic Action (SDA), that held power in the Muslim part of Bosnia, was guilty of physical attacks on opposition activists, beatings of political opponents and persecution of independent media outlets, especially those standing for a multicultural, multi-ethnic, democratic and secular Bosnia-Herzegovina. Western observers were forced to state that the political practice of the SDA was characterized by 'intolerance towards different political views', as well as 'coercive measures to ensure party loyalty'. The ruling party had open links with extremist armed formations and with organized crime. Disagreeing with the authorities was a dangerous business, especially since the party was constantly taking steps to strengthen its positions. 'These steps include firing non-SDA members from leading political and industrial posts, physically assaulting journalists, and discriminating against the non-Muslim population.'[27]

After the West, with the help of a blockade and the bombing of Serbian positions, had forced the Serbian leaders to sit at the negotiating table and sign the Dayton Agreement with the Muslims and Croats, avoiding new elections became impossible. But these 'free and fair' elections, held under the control of Western peace-keepers, took place in a climate of fear. In all three communities, the ruling groups exercised strict control over the situation, denying the opposition any chance to compete freely. Meanwhile it was the opposition, trying somehow to organize itself on a non-ethnic basis, that represented the only chance for a real unification of the country.

The slogan of an 'independent' Bosnia had the ultimate effect of turning Bosnia into a protectorate of the West. The slogan of a single multicultural state led to the rise of a strange formation whose three parts were unwilling and unable to coexist, but were also denied the right to separate from one another. 'One cannot side-step a fundamental question', notes *Labour Focus on Eastern Europe*:

> Is the Bosnian Constitution formally agreed between heads of state at Dayton really a constitution? A sombre and dangerous precedent has been set in the history of international relations: Western creditors have embedded their interests in a constitution hastily written on their behalf, executive positions within the Bosnian state system are to be held by non-citizens who are appointees of Western financial institutions. No constitutional assembly, no consultations with citizens' organisations in Bosnia and Herzegovina, no 'constitutional amendments'[28]

To most Western commentators it seemed obvious that the division of Bosnia would have been an evil, and the preservation of a multinational state a blessing. This was far from obvious to the people living in Bosnia itself. If it had been possible to avoid a civil war through a timely division of the country (as occurred in the case of Czechoslovakia), would this not have been a better solution than attempts to maintain unity at the price of bloodshed? It should also be remembered that the bloody civil war led to division in any case. The Muslim side was opposed to the division, since the Muslim community, which is concentrated mainly in the cities, would have received a disproportionately small share of the territory. The injustice of such a solution is obvious, but the trouble is that 'just' borders do not exist in principle. State borders are defined by relationships of forces and by the process of historical development. These facts also account for the desire to correct previous history with the help of state coercion.[29]

The idea of cultural pluralism is a very attractive one. But it turns out that to achieve this, it would be necessary to compel the Serbs, and in part the Croats, to live in a multinational state. It is quite obvious that a state founded on such coercion could not be democratic. The free elections held in 1996 under the supervision of Western forces could not be intended, and were not intended, to lay the basis for a democratic unified state; they were needed only in order to justify the policies of the Western governments before public opinion in their own countries. 'It would probably be far less painful to allow the Bosnian Serbs to join with the Union Republic of Yugoslavia', observed the Bosnia correspondent of the Moscow daily *Nezavisimaya gazeta*. 'But this is not in the interests of the so-called international community. The path of the forcible unification of, if not of three, then at least two ethnopolitical groups, has created a mass of problems. Some of them are still hidden, but they will most likely break through onto the surface as soon as the existence of this multi-national society becomes a fact.' While forbidding the division of Bosnia, the West could not transform it into a unified nation, and did not try to do so. The people could not and did not want to live together, and did not feel they had any common interests. As *Nezavisimaya gazeta* aptly put it, 'The West has put two spiders in a jar and ordered them to live peacefully together.'[30]

The experience of the USSR also showed that nothing divides people like forced unification. As soon as the force ceases to be applied, the unity is replaced by an outpouring of the hidden enmity that has built up. It is not hard to see that the constant threat of a new explosion can be forestalled only by the permanent presence of outside forces. Foreign occupation thus receives a historical and 'humanitarian' justification. The military and political presence of the Western powers in Eastern Europe is growing, thanks to the fact that conflicts are not being resolved but perpetuated.

The economic and political goals of the West were readily visible both during the Bosnian crisis and during the war in the Persian Gulf. Market reforms have been implemented in the

South at the cost of the destruction of states and the deaths of many thousands of people. In the case of Yugoslavia, the principle of 'divide and rule' proved just as effective as in other imperial wars. The more the local people slaughter one another, the easier (and most importantly, the more respectable) the role of the Western armed forces becomes.

In the epoch of neo-liberalism, 'national liberation' all too often ends up with the emergence of new puppet regimes. Under the conditions of neo-liberal hegemony and of the globalization of capitalism, the Mexican sociologist Adolfo Gilly notes, the traditional programme of national liberation struggle is obsolete. 'Nationalism and anti-imperialism have nothing with which to answer this domination.'[31] Under the new conditions, the rule of transnational capital is imposed through effectively by-passing a weak state. Nationalism, which calls for the fragmenting of federations and multinational states, often becomes a direct ally of neo-liberalism; this is what happened in Eastern Europe. It should not be supposed that this is true of every national movement in the modern world. Nevertheless, the key question today is the social and political essence of the real national movement, not its slogans.

If leftists refuse to support nationalism, this does not by any means signify that they should support 'central' elites against regional ones. In general, the whole purpose of socialists is to resist bourgeois elites at both the central and local levels. But while campaigning against the policies of the British ruling class in Ireland or of the Canadian capitalists in Quebec, or against the aggression by the Russian government in Chechnya, the left has to adopt its own positions, which are distinct from nationalist ones. Otherwise, the very existence of the left makes no political sense.

The Balkans War

If the war in Bosnia provoked disagreements among Western leftists, the NATO attack on Serbia in 1999 saw the beginning of a split no less serious, perhaps, than that which occurred at the beginning of the First World War.

The official pretext for the Western intervention was the persecution by the Serbian authorities of ethnic Albanians, who made up the bulk of the population in the province of Kosovo.

In reality, however, the West felt little concern for the fate of the Albanians. The main provision of the peace agreement offered to the Serbs was for the stationing of NATO forces not only on the territory of Kosovo, but in any part of Serbia and Montenegro, which together make up the new 'rump' Yugoslav Federation. After the Serbian government refused to accept the military occupation of its own country, war became inevitable. Bombs rained down on the cities of Serbia, while the Serbian authorities, acting in the worst Stalinist traditions, began systematically driving Albanians out of Kosovo.

In fact, we were confronted with a classic example of imperialist aggression. To many leftists, however, NATO's war on Yugoslavia was a 'humanitarian mission', undertaken in the name of human rights, in this case, the rights of the Kosovo Albanians. Social democrats, 'greens' and American liberals became the main supporters and ideologues of the war. The crusade against Yugoslav president Milosevic was compared with the struggle against Hitler, though Milosevic, unlike the German dictator, had not attacked anyone outside his borders.

Not only social democrats, but also sections of the radical left applauded the bombings. Meanwhile, the thunderous rhetoric that accompanied the declarations gave proof of the politicians' inner uncertainty. 'It is the duty of the nations that have the military power to protect individual communities from systematic genocide by evil regimes. Where the West has the power and uses it wisely, I will support that intervention', wrote the British parliamentarian Ken Livingstone, leader of the Socialist Campaign Group.[32] The Trotskyist group Workers' Liberty, bitter critics of Livingstone, argued: 'Serbia represents an expansionary dark ages tribalist imperialism and NATO modern civilisation, intervening not to conquer Serbia but, as would-be policemen, to stop the wiping out of the Kosovars.'[33]

By contrast, Livingstone's Socialist Campaign Group colleagues Tony Benn and Alice Mahon sharply condemned the NATO aggression.

Ministers say that this is a war for humanitarian purposes. Can anyone name any war in history fought for humanitarian purposes? Would the Red Cross have done better with stealth bombers and cruise missiles? Of course not. War is about power, for the control of countries and resources.[34]

In Germany, the war was condemned by the Party of Democratic Socialism, the only political force in that country to speak out against NATO. 'You do not avert humanitarian catastrophes with the help of bombs', declared party leader Gregor Gysi. 'On the contrary, you create such catastrophes.'[35] Unlike the pro-NATO leftists, the opponents of the war did not believe in a civilizing 'white man's burden', and did not rejoice at seeing the West take on the functions of world cop. In any case, not everyone who wields a club is a police officer. Police are supposed to act on the basis of the law. NATO's war against Yugoslavia undermined the foundations of international law, and turned the United Nations organization into a cipher. As Gysi and Benn noted, this had been one of the West's main goals in unleashing the war.[36]

Russian leftists, despite all their differences, were united in condemning NATO. Some were even prepared to support Milosevic. 'The present Yugoslav authorities do not suit the NATO countries for ideological reasons', Yevgeniya Polinovskaya wrote in the newspaper of the Russian Komsomol.[37]

The split that has occurred in the left since the beginning of the new Balkans War is strikingly reminiscent of the split that occurred in European social democracy in 1914. It was not only leftists, however, who spoke out against the war. Henry Kissinger and a whole series of American senators, mostly conservatives, condemned it. 'Would we again allow Washington to weaken the world's human rights movements by arousing fears that they will one day mean more bomb-bomb assignments for America?' wrote the conservative commentator A.M. Rosenthal in the pages of the *New York Times*. 'Would we allow ourselves to forget about these people we could indeed help, not with war, but with economic and political pressures against their tormentors?'[38]

Both in the camp of the opponents of the war and in that of its supporters, some quite unexpected partners came together. But in reality, this testified only to the crisis of the left movement, which had lost its traditional values and reference points. The main reason why conservative politicians spoke out against the war was that, unlike the incompetent and irresponsible liberals, they realized how monstrous the consequences of the war would be for the West. The humanitarian catastrophe, when it began, was the result precisely of NATO's military actions. The position of President Milosevic in Serbia was strengthened, and the West was drawn into a conflict from which it could not emerge as a winner. The belief that it was possible to win a war through technological superiority alone was undermined, and, along with it, the ability of the West to intimidate the rest of the world.

Among leftists, meanwhile, emotion had triumphed over political analysis.

It was striking to see how thoroughly the concepts of 'imperialism', 'genocide', 'human rights' and 'self-determination' were trivialized, stripped of any concrete historical and political context. The harsh treatment meted out by the Serbian authorities to the Albanians was not genocide, and it is hard to call people's wish to preserve the integrity of their territory expansionism. Often, protest against the policies of NATO was accompanied by a romantic idealization of the Albanian insurgents of the Kosova Liberation Army, even though these insurgents were collaborating closely with the NATO forces, were involved in smuggling weapons and narcotics, and were systematically terrorizing the peaceful population, including Albanians.

Like the war of 1914–18, the conflict that broke out in the Balkans in 1999 was unjust on both sides. But unlike the situation in 1914, this time there was only one imperialist bloc – NATO. Even while citing the just demands of the Kosovo Albanians, the West was acting in its own interests.[39]

From a moral point of view, the regimes and movements supported by leftists during the national liberation wars of the 1950s and 1960s were often no better than the Milosevic regime in Serbia. In many cases they were worse (the leaders of North Vietnam were Stalinists who systematically repressed their political opponents, while Milosevic had at least been put in office by free elections). The idealization of these regimes was a historic error. But the generation of the 1960s were not mistaken in protesting against the US aggression in Vietnam, since the defeat for imperialism opened up new prospects for democratic and liberating movements throughout the world. Milosevic's nationalism was a cruel and reactionary force. But it was this force that went into battle against the tyranny of the West, while tragically, many left and democratic politicians evaded the fight.

Class or Community?

In the early twentieth century socialists were prepared to speak of wars in which the cause of both sides was unjust. Such wars included not only the Russo-Japanese War, over the division of spheres of influence in China and Korea, but also the Boer War in South Africa. Liberal public opinion in continental Europe was prepared to support the little Boer republics that had come under attack from imperialist Britain (in reality the Boers were the first to take up arms, but this could be explained by the need to strike a 'pre-emptive blow'). From the point of view of the socialists, the Boer republics were European colonial powers in exactly the same way as Britain and France. These republics were founded on the oppression of the indigenous population, that was driven off the land and at times simply exterminated.

The subsequent history of South Africa showed that the scepticism of the socialists was far more justified than the enthusiasm of the liberals. In exactly the same way, the calls to defend little Serbia and Belgium from German aggression in 1914 did not impress Lenin, Martov or Trotsky, who saw very clearly the imperialist interests behind these appeals. Where there were no such interests, the attacks on the small and weak went ahead unpunished.

In the late twentieth century, however, leftists rarely have the intellectual and political boldness to swim against the liberal mainstream, especially where the national question is involved. Protestations of 'love for the weak', if they are not taken as good coin, are at least spared from criticism. Meanwhile, the demands of any nationalist movement are taken seriously, regardless of the forces with which this movement might be linked.

This omnivorousness comes at a price. Wherever the left takes a stance of uncritical solidarity with local nationalist movements, it soon disappears as a political force. Meanwhile, in many countries the left has emerged as a serious national force in direct proportion to the degree to which it has taken its distance from the nationalists. As a historical example one can cite India, where the parting of the ways between communists and nationalists occurred before the conquest of independence, and even though the Indian nationalism of the colonial period had a clearly progressive character.

Northern Ireland provides a contrary example. 'There is a hidden history of class politics in the north of Ireland manifested in both communities', notes the Ulster political scientist Henry Patterson.[40] Here one can cite the activity of the Northern Irish Labour Party and the protest actions mounted by the Protestant working class in the 1960s. This tradition, however, has almost vanished under the impact of Catholic Republican nationalism and Protestant Unionism. In the Irish Republic, the anti-nationalist left tradition is being carried forward by the Democratic Left.

Almost everywhere, the division of political forces along national or community lines has put a stop to serious ideological discussion and has led to the virtual disappearance of the left from political life. In Estonia in the mid-1990s the complaint was voiced continually that the political struggle was bringing about clashes between individuals and groups who shared the same programme. In the republic's parliament, lamented the communist commentator Uno Laht, 'there are people who seem to have been selected at random, who represent no social group and do not answer for anything. They profess no ideology apart from a confused patriotism.' The saddest thing, in Laht's view, is that none of the country's leaders understand the disproportion – that 'without a left political movement there cannot be any real politics. There is no balance of forces. Even if you discard fifty years of history.'[41] Meanwhile the 'independent democrat' Toomas Alatalu has observed ironically that at first all the groups joined in pursuing a right-centrist line, and that then, when their leaders began quarrelling among themselves, 'suddenly some of them turned out to be rightists, and others leftists'.[42]

The 1996 municipal elections in Tallinn, whose population is split more or less evenly between Russians and Estonians, finished up in effect as a contest between the two communities. The problems of the city and society were completely forgotten. The secretary of the ruling Coalition Party told journalists that 'it was not a question of which party wins the election, but rather, of who rules the capital, Estonians or Russians'.[43] For their part, the political leaders of the Russian community called for the retention and strengthening of the 'Russian parties', speaking out against 'wasting strength on a competitive struggle between them, which would be against the interests of all their voters'. The inevitable rivalry, it was said, should be transferred 'from the inter-party to the personal plane'.[44] These parties and candidates all shared a right-centrist bent, and were oriented to one degree or another toward the Moscow authorities. But the desired unity eluded them, precisely because of their lack of principled positions. Where there are no firm principles, personal rivalry and the struggle between group interests hold sway.

It is significant that the 'national card' has been played by the politicians against a background of relatively harmonious coexistence between the two communities on the day-to-day level. Nevertheless, social contradictions, corruption in the structures of power, bureaucratic inefficiency and other problems that have alarmed people in both communities have been forced onto a secondary level. The contradictions between the different communities in the Baltic republics have in turn allowed the Russian authorities to interfere in the affairs of these countries under the pretext of 'defending the rights of Russians'. Meanwhile, the West has been able to play the role of a defender against the 'Russian threat', while at the same time demanding respect for European norms of human rights.

Internationalism

In Ukraine in 1989 there were pro-nationalist and anti-nationalist left currents. By the mid-1990s only the anti-nationalist left held a significant place in political life. In the countries of the former Soviet bloc, a decisive role in the ideological self-realization of the left has been played by the demarcation of leftists from nationalists. Russia has remained an exception; here the official Communist Party has in essence transformed 'anti-imperialist' nationalism into its official ideology. This exception, however, merely confirms the rule. The policies of the communist leadership ultimately led to this half-million-strong party losing influence among the workers, suffering from ideological and programmatic disorientation, and, after its defeat in the elections of 1996, becoming effectively subject to the will of small and uninfluential nationalist groups within the People's Patriotic Union of Russia.

Other leftists, by contrast, have adopted a thoroughly unyielding position with regard to Russian nationalism. Aleksandr Buzgalin has written that nationalism represents a variety of 'conformism', which 'spills over into support for authoritarian, patriarchal, semi-feudal movements'. The national liberation struggle, according to Buzgalin, is progressive only if it 'rests on internationalism'.[45] If Buzgalin and most of the writers grouped around the journal *Al'ternativy* have tried to present a modern interpretation of Leninist principles, Aleksandr Tarasov takes a 'neo-Luxemburgian' approach which has also become common. 'There is no middle ground', Tarasov argues. 'Unless one or another variant of the principle of internationalism ("cosmopolitanism") dominates the collective consciousness of the people, nationalism ("patriotism") will prevail.'[46] In Hungary, similar positions are expressed by Tamas Krausz and the majority of the 'Left Platform' within the Socialist Party. Some Russian leftists have gone even further and in hindsight have condemned the anti-colonial wars in Algeria, Angola and Mozambique, arguing that 'any patriotic or national idea is reactionary'.[47]

Some writers have stressed the existence of a direct continuity between the official Soviet internationalism and subsequent 'national-patriotic' ideologies: 'The former totalitarian state was a school of nationalisms; they were its diligent but not very creative pupils.'[48] This situation has given rise to a further problem; it has become necessary to create a new internationalism, free not only of nationalist ideas, but to an important extent of the heritage of the Soviet past as well. It may be for this reason that Tarasov used the word 'cosmopolitanism', accursed by Soviet ideologues, as a synonym for 'internationalism'.

Neo-Luxemburgian arguments have been a natural reaction to the social-chauvinist ideology of the official Russian Communist Party. But when leftists take their distance from nationalism, this means that they have to formulate their own programmatic demands. For them to advance their own positions means counterposing to the slogans of the nationalists the principles of federalism, decentralization, equal rights, cultural-national autonomy and the solidarity of workers in a single multinational state. The larger this state, and the more multinational and multicultural, the better. But what if part of the population does not want to live in the multinational state?

A part of the Western left tries to sit on two chairs at once, supporting the idea of national statehood for minorities and of a multicultural society. This indicates either the lack of a programme, or the kind of programmatic 'flexibility' that allows one to occupy any position depending on the circumstances. How does a 'prison-house of nationalities' differ from a multi-national state? The difference lies in democracy. What leftists must defend is not the principle of self-determination or that of cultural-ethnic pluralism, but democracy and human rights as such. The only ways of solving the national question that deserve support are those that meet these criteria.

To the idea of the 'national state', leftists need to counterpose their own concept of multinational and multicultural civil society. The programme of socialists has to be based on the principle of equal civil rights, in contrast to the nationalist ideology of 'vertical solidarity' of the masses with 'their' elites. If left-wing tradition presupposes social solidarity and the 'horizontal' unity of workers, nationalism presupposes hierarchy and vertical organization. Leftists and national-conservatives alike see in the state a means of achieving their econcomic goals. But their views of the nature and social purpose of the state are diametrically opposed. This is why leftists and nationalists will never be able to unite successfully, even if they voice similar social demands.

There is not, and cannot be, a single universal principle making it possible to solve national problems. But there can be a single criterion: respect for democratic rights and freedoms. The positions of the left on the national question must be assessed from this point of view as well.

It is clear that as internationalists, leftists must call for the preservation of multinational and multicultural federations. But it is no less clear that the association must be free and voluntary. Meanwhile, the right of peoples to unite with one another has to be respected no less than their right to independence.

The majority of leftists in Russia opposed the dismantling of the Soviet Union not because they were against national independence or the rights of minorities, but because this independence was proclaimed by the republican governments *despite* the clearly expressed wish of the peoples involved. The referendum on the preservation of the Union that was held by the Gorbachev government in March 1991 resulted in a clear majortity for supporters of the Union. Unlike the case with subsequent Russian referendums, no one has ever claimed that normal voting procedures were violated or that the results were falsified. None of the republican governments, except for that of

Ukraine, took democratic measures (such as a new referendum, raising the question of independence during elections and so forth) in order to reconsider the results of this expression of the popular will.

The dissolution of the Soviet Union was a clear violation of the democratic rights of citizens, and was also closely linked to the beginning of the neo-liberal reforms which did away with the system of centralized management and extra-market coordination in the economy of the former USSR. The logic of the struggle for democracy and against neo-liberalism makes leftists supporters of integration. But the tragic pitfall before them is their readiness 'in the name of integration' to show solidarity towards any forces that dream of restoring a unified state. A Russian nationalist who dreams of 'integrating' Belorussia and Chechnya within a police state is no better than a Ukrainian or Belarusian nationalist who bans the publication of books in the Russian language and dreams of reprisals against Jews, Russians and other foreigners. Both, ultimately, are deadly enemies of democratic integration and of the reconciliation of ethnic groups.

The independence struggles of the Chechens or Kurds have deserved the support of leftists not because independent Chechen or Kurdish states represent the best solution in themselves. The reason why these struggles must be supported is that for the majority of the Chechen or Kurdish population, subjected to persecution and genocide, there simply is no other solution in the existing circumstances. It is not that Chechen nationalism is good, and Russian nationalism bad. The democratic principle in any case demands respect for the will of the majority. Even if the majority of the people are wrong in demanding independence, socialists cannot support great-power coercion and repression. But this does not in any way signify that leftists must support a positive programme advanced by nationalists. When nationalism is not a form of defence of democratic rights, it is reactionary through and through. A nationalism which calls for limitations on the civil rights of 'settlers', which denies them equal rights in the use of their language and so on, is anti-democratic in its very essence. Also thoroughly dubious is the idea of supporting a new nationalism as a form of moral recompense for old wrongs (this is very typical of Western leftists who feel a historic guilt for the crimes of the colonial period). Even where the slogan of national statehood represents a form of self-defence, it loses its democratic significance from the moment independence is achieved.

The trouble is that that there are not many situations in the world that are as 'pure' as those of the Chechens or Kurds. Most national movements consist initially of a mix of democratic and anti-democratic elements. But leftists, in order to define their relationship to such movements, analyse the processes involved, and do not mythologize them. The problem is not the supposed weakness of Marxism on the national question, but the unwillingness in this case of leftists to resort to Marxist analysis.

It is precisely because of the political weakness of leftists themselves that national demands are becoming a trap for them. If these demands are just, if they are supported by the majority of workers and are rejected by the ruling class, they can become a legitimate part of the socialist programme. But leftists do not understand the degree to which these slogans are their own, and the degree to which they are not. These demands are ultimately realized without the participation of leftists, and often despite their opposition, giving rise to new injustices along the way. In this respect the position of the left is tragic. In any national struggle, it is doomed to defeat. But this defeat cannot be either decisive or final, since in the final reckoning it is not national but social contradictions that decide how society develops. Every 'victory' in the national struggle simply turns into fresh dramas, until the national contradictions are overtaken by social development. What is catastrophic for leftists is not their inability to solve the national question, but their attempts to give this question a central place in their programme, or to solve it in isolation on the basis of their own ideology. For socialists, the best solution to the national question is to go beyond its boundaries.

4

The Third World Labyrinth: Is a Democratic Model Possible?

Americans have a saying that experience is what you got when you didn't get what you wanted. The peoples of the East and South have tried to catch up with the West, striving for economic success, socialism and democracy. What they have received has been historical experience. Perhaps this is not much of a reward, especially considering the catastrophic price we have paid. Nevertheless, this experience should not be dismissed lightly.

For most of humanity, the twentieth century has been a period of modernization. As we approach the century's end, we can state that all of the projects that have been advanced for global modernization have failed, and that the few instances of success do not change this general picture.

Socialism and Modernization

Traditional oligarchs, capitalists, technocrats and bureaucrats have proven equally incapable of carrying out successful modernization, or at any rate, of ensuring democratic development. From the early years of the twentieth century the idea of modernization has also been seized upon enthusiastically by social democrats, and not only in developing countries. German historians note that even in the era of Karl Kautsky, modernization became the 'kernel' of the social democratic idea, almost an 'ersatz-teleology'.[1]

In this sense, the Russian Bolsheviks were among the best pupils of German social democracy. The conditions of an underdeveloped country were held to require more radical methods and a more rapid pace. The touchstones became the heterogeneity of society and the multi-system character of the economy. The transformation of the state into a monopoly proprietor and the creation of a statocratic system in Russia and China represented the most radical attempts at imposing a 'final solution' to the problems posed by this systemic diversity. The economy was unified into a single entity through the will of an all-powerful bureaucracy. But this was only an apparent synthesis; the integration was never complete, and society never became totally 'homogeneous'. The new mode of production mechanically combined the features of numerous 'conquered' systems from patriarchal feudalism to socialism. An astonishing amalgam appeared; the new system contained everything from slavery in the Stalinist *gulag* and serfdom on the collective farms to the rudiments of genuine self-management. The contradictions of real life in these societies meant that the numerous theoreticians who sought refuge in a face-saving formula ('degenerated workers' state', 'state capitalism', and so on) merely headed into a dead end.

The synthesis was unsuccessful. As the end of the century has neared, the statocratic system everywhere has began disintegrating into its component parts. The crisis of state power has called a new systemic diversity into being, and has returned the societies of Eastern Europe to a state of dependency and backwardness. The bureaucracy, having lost its effectiveness, is reproducing the worst traits of the old ruling classes, and is recreating the type of backward society that should have been banished forever to the past.

'You don't need a microscope to see how similar many of today's individuals and phenomena are to those that were typical of pre-war Europe', wrote the liberal *Moscow News*. 'They never disappeared, but were merely stored away in the freezer of Soviet totalitarianism. Now, with the rise in temperatures, they're thawing out.'[2]

The old problems have returned, as though several decades had been allowed to pass without anything changing, and we are now faced with beginning again from scratch. The same has happened with the many regimes that tried to imitate the 'Soviet model'. After 1989 the radical regimes of the Third World were swiftly transformed, to use the words of John S. Soul, into 'the states of recolonization'.[3]

The promises held out by the 'Western path' have proven to be illusory as well. This 'Western path' has led to the dependency and underdevelopment which in their time gave birth to the Bolshevik Revolution and to numerous revolutionary regimes in the Third World.

Though the neo-liberal world order uses the rethoric of modernization it is not interested in making the whole world equally modern. On the contrary, the coexistence of societies and communities with different levels of modernization remains an important structural factor in this system. It is not just the gap between North and South. As Manuel Castells rightly shows:

> there has also been an accentuation of uneven development, this time not only North and South, but between the dynamic segments and territories of societies everywhere, and those others that risk becoming irrelevant from the perspective of the system's logic. Indeed, we observe the parallel unleashing of formidable productive forces of the informational revolution, and the consolidation of black holes of human misery in the global economy, be it in Burkina Faso, South Bronx, Kamagasaki, Chiapas, or La Courneuve.[4]

However, it is also true that most of these black holes are located in the South and East, not in the North and West. And it is also true that the people living in Burkina Faso or Chiapas are both physically and politically more remote from the centres of the world system than those in South Bronx or La Courneuve.

The problem is not that some countries are less modernized than others, but that capitalism, which proclaims a global modernization, is incapable of ensuring that it is carried out. The young Karl Marx, who together with Engels wrote the *Communist Manifesto*, still believed that the more backward countries, as they were drawn into the capitalist system, would follow the same course as the more developed ones. Rosa Luxemburg was already much less optimistic. In *The Accumulation of Capital*, she argued that when dependent countries became part of the world market, they retained their pre-capitalist structures. These structures, however, were now subject to the logic of capitalist accumulation. The countries involved served as a source of cheap raw materials, and provided additional markets. The periphery of the system was thus doomed to backwardness.

Marxists in the early twentieth century saw the root of the evil as lying in colonial exploitation. But when the countries of Asia and Africa achieved political independence, the dilemma was not solved, and in many cases the situation became even worse. In the 1970s the main problem was considered to be unequal exchange between industrial and agrarian raw material economies. The financial crisis of 1998 showed that despite real advances made by the countries of South-East Asia along the path of industrialization, they had not succeeded in becoming part of the centre. In the 1990s Samir Amin explained the dependence of the periphery in terms of the possession by the countries of the centre of a number of specific monopolies – in the areas of new technology, weapons of mass destruction, the mass information media, and so forth. By the end of the century, however, India, Russia, Pakistan, China and other countries of the periphery had a powerful potential in these areas, and despite this, were unable to make radical changes to their position within the world system.

In reality, whatever form the dependency of the periphery on the centre might assume, its key motivating principle is the very logic of capital accumulation. Capital strives for centralization. After becoming concentrated in the main centres of investment, it is redistributed about the world, including in the direction of the periphery. The more open the economies of the peripheral countries, the more these economies serve the accumulation of capital by the centre. The more developed peripheral countries take part in this redistribution even more actively than the relatively backward ones.

The only structure able to ensure that the investment cycle and the process of accumulation operate in the interests of peripheral societies is the national state. Its advantage lies precisely in the fact that it is not suited to participation in the global process of accumulation, and cannot be an effective player on the capital market. The state inevitably subordinates accumulation and investment policy to the solving of tasks which are its own and which it finds more natural.

This was already grasped by J.M. Keynes:

> I conceive, therefore that a somewhat comprehensive sociali-sation of investment will prove the only means of securing an approximation to full employment; though this need not exclude all manner of compromises. . . . But beyond this no obvious case is made out for a system of socialism.[5]

A consistent socialization of the investment process, meanwhile, inevitably leads us outside the logic of capitalism.

This is why neo-liberal reaction directs such furious attacks against all forms of state participation in the economy, even when this participation is essential for the stability of the bourgeois system itself.

Despite the failures of state planning, it remains an incontrovertible fact that the lower the level of development, the greater the need for the 'statization' of the economy, making possible the implementation of policies aimed deliberately at overcoming backwardness. The fact that statization in South Korea took quite different forms from those it assumed in China is beside the point. Statization of the economy, however, cannot by itself solve the problem. Authoritarian-bureaucratic power structures doom the state sector to inefficiency. The greater the backwardness, the worse the bureaucracy. Backwardness also emerges in the prevalence of barbaric, authoritarian or totalitarian forms of state power. That is why the mixed economy remains an attractive but still vacuous slogan. Without structural reforms in the economy, and without the renewal of the system of state power, the mixed economy simply combines the vices of all the 'models' that have been tried and found wanting. The statization of the economy, while creating the preconditions for accelerated development, simultaneously places obstacles in the way of progress.

In other words, the greater the need for a cure, the less effective the medicine. Socialists, calling for changes in the 'class character' of the state, have been unable to resolve this contradiction, since they have retained their faith in the old Enlightenment concepts. 'Thus socialists were caught up in the centralizing trends of the nineteenth century', observed the American sociologist Robert Dahl:

> Just as liberal reformers turned to the nation-state as the best instrument of reform and regulation, so the socialist leaders placed their hopes, however much their rhetoric sometimes concealed it, on the possibility of using the government of the nation-state to run the economy. Like most reformist liberals, socialists came to see in demands for decentralized institutions of government a mask for privilege and reaction, or the bold, wild face of anarchism, or, like the proposals of Guild Socialists in England, the quaint ideas of academic intellectuals.[6]

Parliamentarism and Authoritarianism

It is possible to move forward only by breaking out of the vicious circle of Enlightenment concepts of power, order and progress. Instead of arguing pointlessly about whether we need a 'big state' or a 'small state', we have to understand that what is necessary is a different state. A radical change in the structures of power is the only alternative to wandering in the labyrinths of authoritarian modernization.

Jorge G. Castaneda, arguing that socialism is dead, maintains that there is a future for leftists in Latin America if they become a force pushing for modernization and state regulation. The place of the revolutionary utopia, he contends, has to be taken by 'legitimacy and flexibility'.[7] However, the socialist alternative in Latin America gained currency precisely because moderate, reformist ideologies of modernization had shown their ineffectiveness. The ideology of 'reform and development' might perhaps be reborn, but it is still not going to work. As critics of Castaneda's book have noted, the rise of social democratic ideology in Latin America has merely reflected the crisis of the revolutionary perspective, 'a mood of disillusionment and anti-utopianism', but in itself this approach 'lacks historical depth and strategic realism'.[8] The call to reject 'utopian' goals is tantamount to demanding abstention from action itself.

If the traditional model of Western parliamentary democracy cannot be mechanically applied under completely different conditions, it does not follow that the peoples of the Third World or Eastern Europe cannot create workable democracies. It is essential to return to democracy its original sense of *people's power*.

It is well known that the parliamentary road to change is far from being the most rapid. No less familiar are the catastrophic results of the numerous attempts, Jacobin and Bolshevik, to speed up the changes, clearing out of the path the democratic 'restrictions' that hindered progress. The history of the Russian soviets in 1917 amounted to an unsuccessful attempt by the masses themselves to resolve this contradiction, creating democratic power of a new type.

Lenin and the Bolsheviks made many speeches praising the concept of a workers' democracy arising spontaneously from below, but this democracy proved incompatible with the Bolshevik concepts of the party and the revolutionary state.

Through recognizing the role of the soviets and resting on the self-organization of the masses, the Bolsheviks were able to take and hold power in the autumn of 1917. But having used the soviets as a springboard to power, the Bolshevik Party was unwilling and unable to renounce its own Jacobin politics. Modern-day leftists who have escaped the hypnotic effect exercised by the Jacobin-Bolshevik tradition will, it must be hoped, prove capable of drawing lessons from this experience.

It is obvious that the model of power that was embodied in the multi-party soviets of 1917 was extremely crude. In many respects the advantages of 'workers' democracy' over parliamentarism were simply the fruit of the imagination of radical ideologues. It was the weakness and ineffectiveness of the soviets that led to the downfall of this form of democracy. The soviets lost their real power because they were unable to defend themselves effectively either against the onslaught of counter-revolution under civil war conditions, or against the Jacobinism of the Bolsheviks.

Nevertheless, if we want to break out of the vicious circle of 'either parliamentarism or authoritarianism', we have to reject the search for simple solutions. All too often, efforts to follow the parliamentary road finish up with the forces involved merely marking time, and sometimes, as the Chilean experience showed, such efforts culminate in the collapse of the institutions of liberal democracy itself. Nonetheless, the alternative to parliamentarism lies not in the dissolving of parliaments, but in the combining of parliaments 'above' with organs of popular power 'below'. In other words, what we need is not soviets instead of parliaments, but soviets in addition to parliaments. It is hardly possible to speak of 'bourgeois' or 'liberal' democracy in the absence of a developed and civilized bourgeoisie, especially when a crisis of democratic institutions is a feature of the West as well. But this does not mean that the people of the Third World or Eastern Europe are doomed to alternating periods of chaos and dictatorship. There is a democratic alternative, but it is not a bourgeois or liberal alternative. In these countries democracy is impossible without a substantial element of socialism. If the public sector plays a decisive role in the economy, if power lies in the hands of workers and their parties, and if self-management is beginning to develop within the state structures, then we are approaching a society in which direct and representative democracy are combined. But even this is not enough. The private sector and transnational corporations cannot merely be counterbalanced by enterprises directly serving the public interest. The very approach taken to development has to be changed.

Capitalist Rationality

In the late nineteenth century Max Weber correctly pointed out that the distinguishing feature of capitalism was not the unbridled pursuit of profit, which occurred in pre-capitalist societies as well, but the planned, rational organization of production for the sake of profit. 'Since there has been no rational organization of labour outside the West, the world's backward countries have not experienced a rational socialism either.'[9]

Participants in the European socialist movement have seen the main contradiction and deficiency of capitalism in the incompatibility between the rational nature of production in each separate factory and the irrational and wasteful anarchy of the capitalist market. Hence their socialist project in essence proposed only the logical completing of the process of economic rationalization begun by capitalism.

Lenin saw the society of the future as one big factory, but forgot to add, 'one big capitalist factory'. It is not surprising that such ideas have been attractive to 'Westernizers' and modernizers in backward countries! Meanwhile, the experience of the twentieth century not only forces us to recognize that attempts at the rational organization of society on the model of the 'big factory' create a monstrous and totally irrational bureaucracy, but, still more important, also demonstrate the narrowness of the capitalist or 'Western' notion of rationality.

Even in Western countries, the idea of social and environmental harmony is more and more often taking over from Enlightenment theories of the rational organization of society. The task now is to give substance to these slogans in the form of real political and economic changes. We will have found the way out of the labyrinth when we come to understand that the main task is not to achieve the highest possible growth rates, but to combine democracy and development, to ensure that every decision that is taken serves to guarantee the rights of the individual. The utopia of the homogeneous society, that has possessed the minds of modernizers of all political persuasions, has to be rejected. To have a democratic perspective means opting for a 'motley society'.

If we sink into chaos as a result of the incompatibility of the socio-economic and political structures present in the country, then the future is grim indeed. But if these structures work together, if each of them experiences its own process of trans-formation and modernization, in parallel with the others and coordinated with them, then this represents a genuine chance. Where the national bourgeoisie has not exhausted its potential, it can also play a certain role in this process.

It is worth recalling Lenin's thoughts on the authoritarian 'Prussian' and democratic 'American' roads of development of capitalism in the countryside. In the former case, capitalist property relations were imposed by the authorities and the oligarchy from above, while in the latter they arose sponta-neously from below. Lenin could hardly have foreseen that the second road would also be possible within the framework of a socialist perspective. Paradoxically, the growth of entrepreneur-ship 'from below' can also represent the outcome of the successful application of socialist measures. The overcoming of dependency, and the banishing of the bureaucratic and comprador capitalist interests that have exploited the country's backwardness and dependency, open up definite opportunities for the development of democratic capitalism. There is inevitably a period of transition, during which the actual movement toward socialism is accompanied by the parallel development of national capitalist entrepreneurship. Ahead lies the promise of progress along several tracks and on several levels, and this is the sole guarantee of genuinely organic development.

Inevitably, numerous transitional forms of democratic economy will appear, such as genuine cooperation and communal property ownership; these will not in their essence be either socialist or capitalist. The role played by the public sector and by the state, which must be in the hands of the workers, is absolutely decisive for the creation of a viable democracy. Only the public sector can create the technological base for disseminating intermediate technologies, and for progressive changes in other sectors. Social ownership can take various forms – state, municipal and cooperative-collective. The decentralization of public property provides a guarantee of dynamic and integrated development that is unattainable either under the sway of private monopolies, or under bureaucratic rule.

Such a strategy is impossible without the implementation of one of the most important of socialist principles – that is, without democratic control over investments. 'The system of private planning and public anarchy, which has become a goal in itself, has to be replaced with new mechanisms of public control over the nation's resources', wrote a British economist. 'This can be realized within a democratic and genuinely mixed economy, in which diverse forms of public control are combined with serious market competition.'[10]

'There is nothing implicitly statist in any struggle for revolutionary change', writes South African socialist Dale McKinley. 'What is implicit, though, is that there must be a fundmental attack on the entrenched economic and political interests of capital (in whatever form) in order for there to be meaningful liberation.'[11] The concentration of a significant part of the social capital in the hands of democratic organs of power at various levels makes it possible to combine a programme of development with a real and not merely a simulated market. Representative organs are desirable precisely because they can exercise administrative control. Their task is to define the general frameworks, goals and priorities that determine the dynamic of the investment process in the public sector.

When the left came to power in South Africa after the fall of apartheid, the question of which strategy of development to apply was transformed from a theoretical question into one of practical politics. The African National Congress government that won the first free elections in April 1994 set out its priorities in the form of a Reconstruction and Development Programme (RDP). While supporting the RDP, the trade unions and the Communist Party stressed that it needed to be 'people-driven'. The basis of this programme had to be mass participation in decision-making, while 'an effective public sector' was required as 'the core and the driving force'.[12] In practice, however, the ANC government has subordinated its activity to the interests of the private sector. The RDP has been transformed into a paradoxical mix of traditional Keynesian measures aimed at stimulating demand through state redistribution, and of neoliberal measures aimed at financial stabilization, the privatization of the state sector and the limiting of expenditures. Riddled with internal contradictions, this strategy, not surprisingly, has proven ineffective.

The shift to the right by the South African government was due mainly to a national and international relationship of forces that was unfavourable to the left. Nevertheless, one is struck by a problem of theory that has the potential to bring about the gradual replacing of a radical by a moderate course, and of a moderate course by a right-wing one. Communists and their allies have shared the traditional idea of a rigid delineation between the 'democratic' and 'socialist' phases of the revolutionary process. This concept proved untrue in practice even in relation to the Russian Revolution of 1917, and has shown itself to be still more inapplicable under modern conditions. While proclaiming the slogan 'Socialism is the Future, Build it Now', the Communist Party has at the same time stressed that it sees the current phase as one of 'advancing, deepening and defending national democratic revolution'.[13] Various concessions have proven necessary and justified for consolidating the 'democratic phase'. However, the task of democratic change is precisely to create socialist institutions which can serve as the core element of further development. Unless this task is carried out, democracy will never be consolidated; the social contradictions of a poor society will either blow it apart, or turn it into an empty farce.

Argentinian sociologist Atilio Boron writes:

> The impoverished and fragmented societies resulting both from the crisis and the response to it – the neoliberal economic restructuring – do not offer most fertile soil for the flowering of democracy. Nor are they factors in upgrading the quality of democratic governance, unless democracy is understood as just the liturgical fulfillment of certain routines and rituals deprived of any substantive meaning.[14]

In the 1990s most Latin American democracies survived but at the price of 'institutional decay', 'progressive loss of content and purpose'.[15]

Beyond 'Models'

The democratization of the economic structures and the dominant position of various types of public property should ensure greater equality, and as a result, a more stable society. Despite the neo-liberal myth, equality is by no means an obstacle to dynamic development even within the context of the capitalist market. The American economists Sam Bowles, David Gordon and Thomas Weisskopf note that Japan is not only an absolute world leader in efficiency, but is also distinguished among the developed capitalist countries by its extremely low inequality of income distribution. 'The message is clear: greater equality can potentially boost economic performance.'[16]

This democratic model is clearly outside the framework of capitalism. The degree to which it is socialist is another question. A distinguishing feature of democratic development is the fact that it occurs 'in one particular country or group of countries' – but only up to a point. The further we proceed along this road, the more we encounter the contradictions of the world market, and the more we place in question the dependency of the periphery on the centre, the more we challenge the hegemony of the transnational monopolies. To jump across historical stages is impossible. The success of anti-capitalist measures creates the illusion of a 'leap to socialism'. Nevertheless, society still passes through this stage, only taking a different route. Of course, it would be desirable to master the achievements of industrial capitalism without, in the words of Marx, having to 'pass through its ghastly peripeteia'.[17] But one has to be extremely cautious. There are times when the Russian proverb, 'The more slowly you travel, the further you get', is borne out. Doing violence to reality not only leads to the degeneration of the revolution, but compromises its ideals on a world scale, and thus plays an objectively reactionary role.

Socialist strategy in a developing country cannot be confined to the solving of immediate problems. It is necessary to solve these problems in such a way as to expedite, as far as possible, the transition to socialism in the next stage of history. Today's task is to prepare for tomorrow, when the 'critical mass' will be reached on the level of the world economy.[18]

A revolutionary regime in a backward country faces three possible variants. These are defeat and the restoration of the old order; degeneration, Thermidor and ultimately, as the Soviet experience showed, bureaucratic restoration; and the consolidation of revolutionary changes through democratic reforms. The last of these roads is the most difficult. It presupposes the rise and survival of a sector of socialist self-management in an economy which retains elements of various systems. The new model of development gives birth to a new model of the class struggle, involving a prolonged struggle by the socialist elements against capitalist and statist ones. Within the structure of the society which is undergoing modernization, the multi-systemic character of society must slowly be overcome. Success in this struggle demands the retention of democratic legality, the unity of the left forces and the hegemony of the proletariat within civil society.

For a long time it was accepted that the main danger faced by a revolution came from its enemies. This is an illusion. The main danger faced by a revolution is inherent in the revolution itself. Revolutions which go too far, perish. But a revolutionary process cannot be halted by decree at a predetermined spot. A revolution has its own logic and its own momentum. Nevertheless the revolutionary process can, and at times must, be redirected onto a reformist track. In such cases there is talk of 'rightward shifts' and of 'deviations', but it is through such methods that the achievements of the revolution can and must be consolidated.[19]

Reformism has to become part of revolutionary strategy. Making the transition from revolutionary ardour to the everyday work of reform is difficult, but it is precisely this which makes it possible to bring reality more closely into accord with the revolutionary ideal. A multi-systemic society requires combined solutions. In a work devoted to Mexico, a US scholar writes that in poor rural districts 'priority has to be given to satisfying basic human needs', while in more developed regions the priority must become 'redistribution with simultaneous growth', and so on.[20] But such a combined strategy in turn demands the creation of a broad democratic bloc, the drawing of the masses into political life, and the transformation of the institutions of power. Without revolutionary resolve, the reformist project will never be implemented. Reformist illusions can therefore prove just as dangerous as revolutionary ones. The only consolation is that the former are less infectious than the latter.

Reformist moods have provided the source for many great revolutionary movements. The onset of revolution occurs at times and in places where the possibilities of reform have been let slip or have been exhausted, or where such possibilities do not exist. Forced to choose between reform and revolution, a society will generally prefer reform, unless mass consciousness is firmly convinced that the revolution will proceed in a peaceful and democratic manner. A substantial section of the Chilean workers in 1970, and of the Russian workers in 1917, were convinced of this. However, their confidence was unjustified. Often, the revolutionary process is perceived by the society itself as a continuation of the struggle for reform. The transition from one phase to the other is often perceptible only in hindsight.

Historical reality, therefore, does not give us the luxury of a choice between revolutionism and reformism. Reformism lacks a purpose unless it is combined with revolutionary perspectives, and revolution without reformist work is equally pointless.

The democratic model is full of contradictions, but this is precisely the reason why it is viable. Within the framework of democracy various paths open up. This is not a condition which has to be endured, but a struggle which must be conducted. Society remains heterogeneous, and reforms reversible. The clash of different forces, and the constant struggle over the choice of a path *even after a particular path has been chosen*, is an inevitable reality of freedom.

In these circumstances a guarantee of democracy and unity, of the integrity of a society which is neither 'monolithic' nor in the process of disintegrating into various segments, is provided by the *socialist* component. The words of Rosa Luxemburg are confirmed for us once again: not only is there no socialism without democracy, but there is no democracy without socialism.

Conclusion

The rule of the New Big Brother is so awful that many people around the world have become nostalgic for the old one. At least the old Big Brother was caring. At least big government could be checked through the rule of law. At least the bureaucracies were accountable to people's representatives in democratically elected parliaments.

The temptation for the left to become nostalgic and conservative is strong and deeply rooted in the minds of millions of working people who form the core constituency of the socialist movement. It is true that their situation has worsened since the introduction of neo-liberal reforms.

But there is no way back. And that is why the neo-liberal global elite is not afraid of the nostalgic left. For those who do not want to be nostalgic the New Big Brother helpfully offers an option of becoming 'modern' through accepting and internalizing the neo-liberal agenda. This kind of left is nothing but another version of the right – more hypocritical and often more corrupt. Some left-wing parties become a coalition of nostalgic dinosaurs and corrupt 'modernists'.

That weakness of political left makes the New Big Brother feel happy and secure. But capitalism cannot escape its own contradictions. The neo-liberal model of capitalism is unstable in principle. Rejecting the criticisms of both Marx and Keynes, and destroying the regulatory structures established under the influence of their ideas, the new world economic order has returned us to the rules of 'classical' capitalism – including over-production and over-accumulation of capital. The main difference from the past is that now we experience the excesses of the free market combined with the excesses of over-centralisation.

Marx was right when he insisted that these contradictions logically led to revolution. But where are the revolutionaries? Where is the revolutionary project?

The crisis of 1998 made many mainstream economists change sides. They started speaking about capital controls or 'international Keynesianism'. This is nothing new either. The institutions which in the 1980s and 1990s imposed global capitalist deregulation on the nations were originally created as Keynesian. This is true in the case of the International Monetary Fund or the World Bank. It is also true in the case of the European Union and its structures.

Regulation remains an empty word unless the power of the New Big Brother is undermined politically and economically. That can be done and must be done internationally but through nation-states. The left must not just fight to conquer the state but first of all to transform it. That was the core idea of the original Marxist project and it is as valid today as it was hundred years ago. The state is weakened by the neo-liberal model – so we must use its weakness in our struggles.

We do not fight for more state or less state but for a different state. The network society will not emerge as a result of capitalist evolution but it can become a product of socialist transformation. We must recreate the public sector as decentralized and democratic, connected to community and accountable. We must re-establish the social security system on the basis of self-organization and representation. And society must penetrate the state as deeply as possible.

The left must reinvent the state – based on social networks, participation and citizenship, as opposed to the totalitarian hierarchies of the corporate Big Brother and multinational capitalist giants.

New Big Brother has to be stopped.

That can be achieved through class struggle and through expropriation of big corporations. If we are afraid of thinking in these terms we are doomed to defeat politically and morally. Is the left capable of responding to the challenges it faces? Maybe it is not. But in this case the loser will not be just the socialist movement but the humanity as a whole.

The struggles already go on, the task is to coordinate them and to give the common perspective. That means to be universalist and patriotic at the same time. And quite possibly these struggles will reshape national identities the same way as the great patriotic and internationalist struggles did in the nineteenth century.

The time of change is only beginning. The battlefield is the whole planet. The stake is the future of the humankind. And for the working people there is a world to win.

Notes

Introduction: The New Big Brother

1. J. Brecher and T. Costello. *Global Village or Global Pillage?* Boston, 1994, p. 62.
2. Ibid., p. 63.
3. *Monthly Review*, 50 (4), September 1998, p. 2.
4. *Green Left Weekly*, 14 October 1998, p. 15.
5. Manuel Castells. *The Information Age, vol. I: The Rise of the Network Society*. Oxford and Malden, 1998, p. 192.
6. J. Brecher and T. Costello, *Global Village*, p. 54. See also B. Harrison. *Lean and Mean: The Changing Landscape of Corporate Power in the Age of Flexibility*. New York, 1994, pp. 9, 127, 171.
7. Manuel Castells. *The Information Age, vol. I*, p. 474.

1   The State and Globalization

1. *Svobodnaya mysl'*, 1995, no. 8, p. 60.
2. Ibid., p. 61.
3. I. Wallerstein. *Unthinking Social Science*. Cambridge, 1991, p. 57.
4. *Links*, July–October 1996, no. 7, p. 60. If we look at Kondratiev's long waves of capitalist development we see a similar picture. During the upswings in the long cycles we see the expansion of the state (military, geographic and often economic). During the periods of decline we see that exchange and communication technologies develop faster than industrial production. Exactly as Kondratiev predicted, the periods of expansion are accompanied by revolutions, wars and social change, while the periods of decline are accompanied by political reaction (see N.D. Kondratiev. *Problemy economicheskoi dinamiki*. Moscow, 1989, pp. 197, 199, 201–5; see also S. Bowles, D. Gordon and Th. Weisskopf. *After the Waste Land*. London, 1990, p. 18). According to Kondratiev great technological innovations characterize the end of the decline phase. Using Kondratiev's cycles as the framework of analysis we easily come to conclusion that the end of 1990s is the final stage of the long wave of decline, which started in the 1970s. That means that we are entering into the new phase of capitalist development, which will not only lead to economic expansion based on new technologies

but also will be a time of social upheaval, revolutions and the growing role of the state.

5. *Links*, July–October 1996, no. 7, p. 61. See also Chris Harman. 'Globalisation: a critique of a new orthodoxy.' *International Socialism*, Winter 1996, no. 73. According to Harman, the ideology of globalization is playing a significantly greater role in the class struggle than the globalization of productive links.
6. *Rabochaya politika*, 1996, no. 6, p. 42. Other authors are even more articulate. Ellen Meiksins Wood writes:

> In a way, the whole point of 'globalization' is that competition is not just – or even mainly – between individual firms but between whole national economies. And as a consequence, the nation-state has acquired new functions as an instrument of competition. If anything, the nation-state is the *main agent* of globalization. U.S. capital, in its quest for competitiveness, demands a state that will keep social costs to a minimum, while keeping in check the social conflict and disorder generated by the absence of social provision. (*Rising from the Ashes? Labor in the Age of 'Global' Capitalism.* Ed. by E. Meiksins Wood, P. Meiksins, M. Yates. New York, 1998, p. 12).

7. *Green Left Weekly*, 26 March 1997, p. 21.
8. See the discussion of integration in the books: *Pyat' let Belovezh'ya. Chto dal'she?* Moscow, 1997; A. Vygorbina. 'Dva podkhoda k sblizheniyu.' *Nezavisimaya gazeta-Stsenarii*, 15 May 1997.
9. *Nezavisimaya gazeta*, 15 May 1997.
10. The American economist Doug Henwood has shown that the picture of transnational companies as 'global assembly lines' is also exaggerated. Compared with 1977, the inter-firm transfer of partly finished goods to or from foreign manufacturing affiliates has increased from 12 per cent of US trade to. . . 13 per cent! It is true that the share of US GDP represented by trade rose during this period from 17 to 24 per cent, but it nevertheless remains less than in other countries. Inter-firm transfers of the global assembly line type rose from 2 per cent in 1977 to 3.2 per cent in 1994 (see *Left Business Observer*, 14 May 1997, no. 77). In other words, the globalization of real production is uneven (it is less in large countries with developed internal markets), and on the whole is significantly less than ideologues have assumed.
11. *L'Événement du jeudi*, 1996, no. 617, p. 47.
12. *New Left Review*, March–April 1996, no. 216, p. 74.
13. S. Amin. *Re-Reading the Postwar Period: An Intellectual Itinerary.* New York, 1994, p. 207.
14. Ibid., p. 211.

15. S. Clarke. *Keynesianism, Monetarism and the Crisis of the State.* Aldershot, 1988, p. 358.
16. P. Ingrao, R. Rossanda et al. *Verabredungen zum Jahrhundertende. Eine Debatte uber die Entwicklung des Kapitalismus und die Aufgaben der Linken.* Hamburg, 1996, p. 193.
17. Ibid., pp. 202–3.
18. Ibid., p. 197.
19. At the international conference 'Globalization and Citizenship', held in Geneva in December 1996 under the sponsorship of the United Nations Organization, it was noted that:

    Although pressures from international civil society and inter-ventions by intergovernmental organizations have broadened the range of rights and standards historically associated with citizenship, far less has been achieved at the level of enforcement. Indeed it would seem that the weakening of state structures in many countries has seriously undermined the possibility of enforcing global standards. (*UNRISD News*, Autumn 1996/Winter 1997, no. 15, pp. 1–2).

20. *Economist*, 7–13 October 1995, Special supplement, p. 9.
21. S. Clarke, *Keynesianism*, p. 355.
22. W. Bello, Sh. Cunningham and Li Kheng Poh. *A Siamese Tragedy. Development and Disintegration in Modern Thailand.* London and New York, 1998, p. 39.
23. See P. Ingrao and R. Rossanda. *Appuntamenti di fine secolo.* Rome, 1995; P. Ingrao, R. Rossanda et al., *Verahredungen zum Jahrhun-drertende.*
24. W. Hutton. *The State We're In.* London, 1996, p. xxiii.
25. Ibid., p. 342.
26. *New Left Review*, May–June 1996, no. 217, p. 4.
27. *Utopie-kreativ*, March 1997, no. 77, p. 94; H.-J. Stadermann. *Wie der EURO kommt.* Marburg, 1996, pp. 25, 53.
28. *Moscow Times*, 19 December 1996.
29. Patrick Viveret in *Iniciativa Socialista*, February 1997, no. 43, p. 52.
30. S. Clarke, *Keynesianism*, p. 356.
31. See Daniel Hellinger and Dennis R. Judd. *The Democratic Facade.* Belmont, CA, 1994, p. 329.
32. W. Hutton, *The State We're In*, p. 17.
33. C. Lasch. *The Revolt of the Elites and the Betrayal of Democracy.* New York and London, 1996, p. 197.
34. L.C. Thurow. *The Future of Capitalism.* New York, 1996, p. 242.
35. *Korea Focus*, March–April 1997, vol. 5, no. 2, pp. 117, 119.
36. *Baltic Times*, 1996, no. 19, p. 4.
37. *Vechernie vesti* (Tallinn), 1996, no. 177, p. 8.
38. *Estoniya*, 2 August 1996.
39. *Kupecheskaya gavan'*, 2 August 1996, no. 31, p. 3.

40. *Svobodnaya mysl'*, 1997, no. 1, pp. 45–6. On similar trends in the Third World see: K. Kuverakorn. 'Let's understand the causes of conflicts clearly.' *Nation*, Bangkok, 21 March 1999.
41. *Svobodnaya mysl'*, 1997, no. 1, p. 45.
42. *Viento del Sur*, winter 1996, no. 8, p. 3.
43. Ibid., p. 57.
44. This is how the connection between globalization and the reform of the state is interpreted in documents of the German Party of Democratic Socialism. See *Alternative Politik und Globalisierung*. PDS International, Informationsschrift der AG Friedens- und Internationale Politik. Extra. Berlin, S.D., pp. 11–13.
45. *Links*, July–October 1996, no. 7, p. 54.
46. *Financial Times*, 15 September 1998.
47. *Moscow Times*, 15 September 1998.
48. *Journal of Commerce*, 3 September 1998.
49. *Financial Times*, 15 September 1998.

2   Is Nationalization Dead?

1. *Mapping the West European Left*. Ed. by P. Anderson and P. Camiller. London and New York, 1994, pp. 20–1.
2. *PDS Pressedienst*, 1995, no. 28.
3. Quoted in *Socialist Campaign Group News*, April 1996, p. 2.
4. Ibid. R. Miliband also stresses the link between the effectiveness of regulation and nationalization: 'Regulation of private business, in a democratic context, has a limited and uncertain reach. Public ownership avoids most of the problems which regulation encounters: the latter is no substitute for the former' (R. Miliband. *Socialism for a Sceptical Age*. Cambridge, 1994, p. 103). Under conditions of the globalization of capitalism, a strong state sector remains the sole basis for serious regulation.
5. Will Hutton, *The State We're In*. p. xxii.
6. Ibid., pp. 298, 326.
7. Ibid., p. 50.
8. *Socialist Review* (San Francisco), 1995, vol. 25, no. 3–4, p. 20.
9. Ibid., p. 21.
10. R. Morrison. *We Build the Road as we Travel*. Philadelphia, 1991, pp. 222, 223.
11. *Al'ternativy*, 1996, no. 2, p. 110.
12. Ibid., p. 112.
13. A.I. Kolganov. *Kollektivnaya sobstvennost' i kollektivnoe predprinimatel'stvo*. Moscow, 1993, p. 136.
14. Ibid., p. 153.

15. M. Chumachenko. 'Country Report on Transformation of Ukraine.' Paper prepared for 3rd AGENDA Workshop on Lessons from Transformation, 12–14 April 1996, Vienna, p. 14.
16. A.I. Kolganov. *Kollektivnaya sobstvennost' i kollektivnoe predprinimatel'stvo*, pp. 75, 87.
17. *Svobodnaya mysl'*, 1994, no. 4, p. 73. An analysis of the fact that under the conditions of the market economy the holding of property by workers leads to the intensification of exploitation and to the growth of conflict is made using the example of the American company United Airlines. See the article by R. Lesnik and M. Miah. '"Employee Ownership": A Blow to Unionism.' *Independent Politics*, Fall 1994, no. 7.
18. *Al'ternativy*, 1996, no. 2, p. 108.
19. A.I. Kolganov. *Kollektivnaya sobstvennost' i kollektivnoe predprinimatel'stvo*, p. 155.
20. V. Belotserkovskiy. *Obshchestvo samoupravleniya – spasenie i rastsvet Rossii*. Moscow, 1994, p. 13.
21. D. Sassoon. *One Hundred Years of Socialism*. London and New York, 1996, p. 711.
22. *New Left Review*, September–October 1996, no. 219, pp. 42–3.
23. *Svobodnaya mysl'*, 1994, no. 4, p. 75.
24. D.M. Kotz with F. Weir. *Revolution from Above*. London and New York, 1997, p. 39.
25. D. Sassoon, *One Hundred Years of Socialism*, p. 756.
26. R. Miliband, *Socialism for a Sceptical Age*, p. 55.
27. S. Kikeri, J. Neelis and M. Shirley. *Privatization: The Lessons of Experience*. World Bank, Washington, DC, 1992, p. 3. Andor and Summers comment:

    It is true that privatized firms are often more profitable than when under public ownership, this does not however imply that public firms have been mismanaged. It is more commonly the case that public firms simply have lower regulated profits, to the benefit of consumer. (L. Andor, M. Summers. *Market Failure: A Guide to Eastern 'Europe's Miracle'*. London, 1998, p. 89).
28. P. Cook and C. Kirkpatrick (eds) *Privatisation in Less Developed Countries*. London, 1988, p. 9.
29. C. Adam, W. Cavendish and P. Mistry. *Adjusting Privatization: Case Studies from Developing Countries*. London, 1992. In theory privatization has to increase competition in the economy thus bringing down prices (and wages as well). However Eastern European as well as Western experience proves that in practice it does not work this way. 'Frequently privatizations have been concluded with significantly diminished competetion such as the notorious aquisition of the Hungarian firm Tungsram by General Electric', write Andor and Summers (Andor and Summers, *Market Failure*, p. 89).

30. B. Martin. *In the Public Interest?* London, 1993, p. 146.
31. On British privatization see Andor and Summers, *Market Failure*, pp. 90–2. Gladstone Hutchinson, in his essay on British privatization, presents the results more positively, but he also agrees that in some industries the ownership arrangement 'had little impact on performance' (G. Hutchinson. *Efficiency Gains through Privatization of UK Industries. Privatization and Economic Efficiency. A Comparative Analysis of Developed and Developing Countries.* Ed. by Attirat F. Ott and Keith Hartly. Aldershot, 1991, p. 97). A report by the Institute of Economics of the Russian Academy of Sciences, prepared in 1995 by authors holding moderately liberal views, states that despite widespread privatization in the developed capitalist countries, the share of the state sector in Gross Domestic Product 'remains significant, especially in Europe'. The report also notes a sharp rise in efficiency as a result of 'the introduction of the principles of market competition'. In the view of the report's authors, 'state property reflects a different system of interests and in many ways expresses different relationships than it did some decades ago' (*Svobodnaya mysl'*, 1996, no. 4, p. 8). The authors of the report, who are far from being socialists, see the future of the state sector much more optimistically than most left-wing politicians.
32. *Nezavisimaya gazeta*, 11 April 1996. On general results of privatization in Eastern Europe see Andor and Summers, *Market Failure*, pp. 92–9.
33. Yu. Luzhkov. *My deti tvoi*, Moskva. Moscow, 1996, pp. 284, 285.
34. Ibid., p. 288.
35. *Svobodnaya mysl'*, 1996, no. 4, p. 42. A case study devoted to municipal contruction projects in Great Britain showed that, despite the triumph of Thatcherism, in Britain during the 1980s public investments in a number of cases provided 'an enormous return' (R. Hackney. 'Community Enterprise and How to Give Inner Cities New Life.' In: *Cities of Europe: The Public Role in Shaping the Urban Environment.* Ed. by T. Deelstra and O. Yanitsky. Moscow, 1991, p. 216). Construction projects undertaken by local authorities with the active participation of the population not only provide income for the city and housing for the community, but 'stop people being unemployed' (Hackney, 'Community Enterprise', p. 221). It is quite a different matter that efficient municipal enterprises represent a threat to private profits.
36. *Nezavisimaya gazeta*, 15 June 1996.
37. *Moskovskiy komsomolets*, 31 January 1997.
38. *Finansovye izvestiya*, 4 April 1996, no. 36.
39. *Moscow Tribune*, 9 July 1996.

40. *Svobodnaya mysl'*, 1996, no. 8, p. 71. The growth of public sector 'from below' is not just a Russian phenomenon. One can see a manifestation of the same trend represented by the public development authoroties in the United States. Steel Valley Authority was established by ten towns in the Pittsburgh area with the power to float bonds, own and manage enterprises. Another example is Connecticut Community Economic Development Program, created by the state government in the 1990s. See J. Brecher, T. Costello, *Global Village or Global Pillage?* Boston, 1994, p. 62, p. 181.
41. *Baltic Times*, 1996, no. 19, p. 23.
42. P. Mertlik. 'Czech Privatization: From Public Ownership to Public Ownership in Five Years.' Paper prepared for 3rd AGENDA Workshop on Lessons from Transformation, 12–14 April 1996, Vienna, pp. 8–9. It is interesting to mention that in 1997–98, when the economic situation deteriorated, the same commentators who had praised the Czech Prime Minister Vaclav Klaus as a 'model reformer' suddenly discovered that there was 'not enough' privatization, the industry 'has not gone through a fundamental restructuring' and remained 'dependent on the quasi-state-run banking system' (*Transitions*, vol. 5, no. 4, April 1998, p. 54).
43. A. Zwass. *From Failed Communism to Underdeveloped Capitalism.* London, 1995, p. 198.
44. *International Socialism*, Spring 1998, no. 78, p. 49.
45. M.G. Chumachenko. 'Dopovid' o problemakh trasformatsii v Ukraini.' Paper prepared for 3rd AGENDA Workshop on Lessons from Transformation, 12–14 April 1996, Vienna, pp. 17–18. Another Ukrainian economist stresses that the decline of production was faster and crisis was deeper in the sectors where the percentage of privatized enterprises was higher (Yu. Buzdugan. 'Sotsial-demokratychny vybir, kn. 1: Postindustrial'na sistema Ukrainy.' Kiev, 1997, manuscript, p. 22).
46. See *Al'ternativy*, 1995, no. 4, p. 116.
47. *After the Market Shock. Central and East-European Economies in Transition.* Ed. by M. Perczinski, J. Kregel and E. Matzner. Aldershot, 1994, p. 234.
48. *Economic Survey of Europe in 1991–92.* Geneva. Economic Commission of Europe, 1992. Quoted by Kowalik and Bugaj in Perczinski et al. (eds) *After the Market Shock*, p. 234.
49. *Svobodnaya mysl'*, 1996, no. 8, p. 61.
50. See R. Miliband, *Socialism for a Sceptical Age*, pp. 103–7.
51. *Monthly Review*, July–August 1996, vol. 48, no. 3, p. 61.
52. M. Castells. *The Information Age*, vol. 1, p. 60.
53. Ibid.
54. B. Martin, *In the Public Interest?*, p. 194.

55. For many scholars the failures of the neo-liberalism have aroused hopes that good sense will triumph. In his book *In the Public Interest?*, B. Martin expresses hopes in the advent to power in Washington of the Clinton administration:

    There is growing awareness, too (and not only in the White House), that far from being a drain, public investment, including on services such as education and health, but not only on those sectors, can be the engine of economic recovery and can mobilize initiative and enterprise to make gains in both efficiency and quality (B. Martin, *In the Public Interest?*, p. 199).

    However, the Clinton administration has not justified the hopes that were placed in it. This was only to be expected; in questions of property, the decisive factor is not good sense, but social interests.
56. L.C. Thurow, *The Future of Capitalism*. p. 290.
57. Ralph Miliband notes that the rejection of the idea of nationalization cannot be considered a consequence of globalization: 'the ideological shift. . . occurred well before the growth of multinational companies' (R. Miliband, *Socialism for a Sceptical Age*, p. 103). In fact, globalization itself became possible thanks to the successes of national states in developing information technologies, infrastructures, education and so forth, which would have been impossible without a strong public sector.
58. Ibid., pp. 289, 291.
59. Ibid., p. 295.
60. *OCAW Reporter*, July–August 1996, vol. 52, no. 5–6, p. 16.
61. Alec Nove wrote on the socialization of consumption in a discussion with Ernest Mandel on the pages of *New Left Review*. In Nove's view socialization was indispensable in such sectors as health, education, public housing, urban public transport and communications (*New Left Review*, January–February 1987, no. 161, p. 102). Miliband also writes of the need for the 'decommodification of consumption' (R. Miliband, *Socialism for a Sceptical Age*, pp. 117–18).
62. *Beyond Keynesianism. The Socio-Economics of Production and Full Employment*. Ed. by E. Matzner and W. Streek. Aldershot, 1991, p. 31.
63. Perczinski et al. (eds) *After the Market Shock*, pp. 128, 122, 127.
64. The fear of speaking of *real* alternatives, however, generates new utopias about 'progressive' solutions combining the best elements of both non-statist socialism and liberalism through a charted course between social-democracy and neo-liberalism. For example Roberto Mangabeira Unger argues that in rich and poor countries alike, a more decentralized and inclusive rela-

tionship can be built between business and government and that can lead us to a 'real' and 'progressive' democracy (see R. Mangabeira Unger. *Democracy Realized. The Progressive Alternative*. London, 1998). Two things remain unclear here: does the author really believe all that, and why is he considered to be a left-wing political theorist?
65. *Le Monde Diplomatique*, June 1996, p. 9.
66. *Monthly Review*, July–August 1996, vol. 48, no. 3, pp. 60–1.

3   Nations and Nationalism

1. I.V. Stalin. *Sochineniya*, vol. 2, p. 296.
2. Ibid., vol. 11, pp. 333–5.
3. B. Anderson. *Imagined Communities*. London and New York, 1989.
4. *Svobodnaya mysl'*, 1996, no. 1, p. 58.
5. See E. Gellner. *Nations and Nationalism*. Oxford and Cambridge, MA, 1983; E.J. Hobsbawm. *Nations and Nationalism since 1870*. Cambridge, 1990; Anderson, *Imagined Communities*.
6. E. Balibar and I. Wallerstein. *Race, Nation, Class*. London and New York, 1991, p. 81.
7. *Green Left Weekly*, 8 November 1995, no. 210, p. 23.
8. *War Report*, October 1995, no. 37, p. 15.
9. R. Rosdolsky. *Engels and the 'Nonhistoric' Peoples: The National Question in the Revolution of 1848*. Glasgow, 1986, p. 129.
10. *Panorama*, Moscow, May 1992, no. 2, p. 12.
11. E. Balibar and I. Wallerstein, *Race, Nation, Class*, p. 82.
12. R. Alapuro. *State and Revolution in Finland*. Berkeley, L.A. and London, 1988, pp. 97–8.
13. *New Left Review*, May–June 1996, no. 217, p. 43.
14. V.I. Lenin. *Polnoe sobranie sochineniy*, vol. 25, p. 275. It is possible that Lenin's position on self-determination was also influenced by the events of 1917 in Finland. Its independence was proclaimed on 6 December and recognized by the Bolshevik government at the Finns' request, three weeks later. That was followed by a short civil war in Finland. The Reds got no support from Russia and the reign of White terror broke out.

    During the first week after the war the Whites executed an average 200 people a day, and the total number of Reds executed in the last weeks of the war and immediately thereafter rose to about 5,600. In addition, roughly 12,500 persons died in prison camps, in which the victors incarcerated about 82,000 people. In a country of 3.1 million people, the executions and camp deaths were so extensive that they exceeded, both relatively and absolutely, the contemporaneous ones in Hungary. (R. Alapuro, *State and Revolution in Finland*, p. 177)

After that Lenin reasonably came to the conclusion that the issue of national independence should not be disconnected from that of class struggle.

15. R. Abraham. *Rosa Luxemburg*. Oxford, New York and Munich, 1989, p. 97.
16. Ibid.
17. *Baltic Times*, 1996, no. 19, p. 1.
18. *Nezavisimaya Gazeta*, 11 June 1996, p. 7.
19. *War Report* (Institute of War and Peace Reporting, London), November–December 1996, no. 47. p. 38.
20. *Nezavisimaya Gazeta*, 21 December 1996, p. 3.
21. *War Report*, November–December 1996, no. 47, p. 39.
22. Ibid., p. 28.
23. For a more detailed treatment of national liberation movements and simulated revolutions, see B. Kagarlitsky. *The Mirage of Modernization*. New York, 1995.
24. *Socialist Campaign Group News*, October 1995, p. 8.
25. *Labour Focus on Eastern Europe*, Summer 1996, no. 54, p. 14.
26. Ibid., p. 15.
27. *War Report*, October 1995, no. 37, p. 6.
28. *Labour Focus on Eastern Europe*, Summer 1996, no. 54, p. 27.
29. The best-known attempt to bring state frontiers into accordance with the demographic ratios between various nationalities in Europe was Hitler's pursuit of '*Lebensraum*' for the German people. It is unfortunate that many left-wing commentators on the Bosnian crisis have put forward analogous arguments.
30. *Nezavisimaya gazeta*, 20 September 1996, p. 4.
31. *Utopie Critique*, 1997, no. 9, p. 71.
32. *Socialist Campaign Group News*, April 1999, p. 7.
33. *Workers' Liberty*, April 1999, p. 4.
34. *Socialist Campaign Group News*, April 1999, p. 6.
35. *PDS Pressedienst*, 1999, no. 13, S. 5.
36. See *PDS Pressedienst*, 1999, no. 13, S. 4; *Socialist Campaign Group News*, April 1999, p. 6.
37. *Novosibirskii komsomolets*, March–April 1999, p. 3.
38. *New York Times*, 16 April 1999, p. A25.
39. On KLA recruiting people at gunpoint see *Newsweek*, 12 April 1999, p. 33, on their connection to drug trade and their ties with NATO see the *New York Times*, 4 April 1999, p. 8. For a positive view of the KLA see Michael Karadjis. 'What is the KLA?' *Green Left Weekly*, 12 April 1999. However, even Karadjis, who is almost uncritically supportive of the KLA, recognizes the criminal connection: 'when arms arrived from Albania in 1997, some were obtained by organised criminals, who terrorised local

Albanians and Serbs alike, especially in the border areas' (*Green Left Weekly*, 12 April 1999, p. 16).

40. *Workers' Liberty*, March 1996, no. 29, p. 10.
41. *Molodezh' Estonii*, 1 August 1996.
42. *Den' za dnem*, 2 August 1996.
43. *Baltic Times*, 1996, no. 19, p. 4.
44. *Estonia*, 2 August 1996; *Molodezh' Estonii*, 1 August 1996.
45. A.V. Buzgalin. *Budushchee kommunizma*. Moscow, 1996, p. 49.
46. *Panorama*, May 1992, no. 2, p. 12.
47. *Al'ternativy*, 1994, no. 1, p. 91.
48. *Svobodnaya mysl'*, 1994, no. 5, p. 37.

4 The Third World Labyrinth: Is a Democratic Model Possible?

1. *Die Freiheit der Andersdenken. Rosa Luxemburg und das Problem der Demokratie*. Hrsg. Von Th. Bergmann, J. Rojahan, F. Weber. Hamburg, 1995, pp. 47–8.
2. *Moskovskie novosti*, 16 June 1991, no. 24, p. 10.
3. *Socialist Register 1993*. Ed. by R. Miliband and L. Panitch. London, 1993, p. 154.
4. M. Castells. *The Information Age*, vol. I, Oxford and Malden, 1998, p. 2.
5. J.M. Keynes. *General Theory of Employment, Interest and Money*. Macmillan, London, 1953, p. 378.
6. R.A. Dahl. *After the Revolution? Authority in a Good Society*. New Haven and London, 1990, p. 106.
7. Jorge G. Castaneda. *Utopia Unarmed*. New York, 1993. Cited from the Spanish-language edition: *La Utopia desarmada*. Mexico, 1993, p. 563. For a detailed criticism of Castaneda's views, see the article by J. Petras and S. Vieux. 'Pragmatism Unarmed.' *Links*, January–April 1996, no. 6.
8. *Links*, January–April 1996, no. 6, p. 63.
9. M. Weber. *Izbrannye proizvedeniya*. Moscow, 1990, p. 52.
10. R.J. Barnet. *The Lean Years*. London, 1981, p. 312. For a historical survey of the discussion on socialism, planning and the simulated market see R. Blackburn. 'Fin de Siècle: Socialism after the Crash', *New Left Review*, 1991, no. 185.
11. D. McKinley. *The ANC and the Liberation Struggle*. London and Chicago, 1997, p. 131.
12. *Links*, January–April 1996, no. 6, p. 124.
13. Ibid., p. 116.
14. A. Boron. *State, Capitalism and Democracy in Latin America*. London, 1995, p. 211.
15. Ibid., p. 215.

16. S. Bowles, D. Gordon, T. Weisskopf, *After the Waste Land*. London, 1990, pp. 222–4.
17. K. Marx and F. Engels. *Sochineniya*. vol. 19, p. 401.
18. Lenin believed that revolution would take place at the 'weak link' of the capitalist world system. But after the 'front' of capitalism has broken at such a weak link, the revolution finds itself in a critical situation. The weak link of capitalism turns into a weak link of socialism. Both Lenin and Trotsky sensed this contradiction, but they were unable to resolve it.
19. A fresh evaluation of Lenin's New Economic Policy, as a reformist opportunity that was let slip, might be made from this standpoint.
20. D. Goulet. *Mexico: Development Strategies for the Future*. Notre Dame and London, 1983, pp. 113–14.

Index